D1305805

Dinah Zike's

Big Book of
United States History

Middle School and High School

Dinah Zike, M.Ed.

Lara

Copyright ©2004, Dinah-Might Adventures, LP
Dinah-Might Adventures, LP
P.O. Box 690328
San Antonio, Texas 78269-0328
Office (210) 698-0123
Fax (210) 698-0095
Orders only: 1-800-99DINAH (993-4624)
Orders or catalog requests: orders@dinah.com
E-mail: dma@dinah.com
Website: www.dinah.com
ISBN 1-882796-24-1

Table of Contents

Dear Teacher:

What is a Foldable?

In this book you will find instructions for making Foldables as well as ideas on how to use them. A Foldable is a 3-D, interactive graphic organizer. Making a Foldable gives students a fun, hands-on activity that helps them organize and retain information.

I first began inventing, designing, and adapting Foldables over thirty years ago. Today, I present Foldable workshops and keynote addresses to over 50,000 teachers and parents a year. Students of all ages are using my Foldables for daily work, note-taking activities, student-directed projects, as forms of alternative assessment, journals, graphs, charts, tables, and more. You may have seen at least one of the Foldables featured in this book used in supplemental programs or staff-development workshops.

After workshop presentations, participants would often ask me for lists of activities to be used with the Foldables they had just learned to make. They needed help visualizing how Foldables could be used to display the data associated with their disciplines—in this case, United States History. So, over twenty-five years ago, I started collecting and sharing my ideas about how Foldables could be used to meet the needs of the history teacher.

This book is the fruit of those years. It is organized in four parts. The first part introduces Foldables, explaining how they work and some of the ways they can be used. The second part gives step-by-step instructions on how to make 35 basic Foldable activities, along with practical classroom-tested tips. The third part of the book presents suggestions for using Foldables with specific United States History topics, and the fourth section consists of reproducible graphics which can be used with Foldables and other projects.

Workshops
Contact Cecile Stepman
1-210-698-0123
cecile@dinah.com

Orders
1-800-99DINAH
orders@dinah.com

E-Group
Join on website: www.dinah.com
or e-mail mindy@dinah.com

Why Use Foldables in Social Studies?

When teachers ask me why they should take time to use the Foldables featured in this book, I explain that they

. . . quickly organize, display, and arrange information, making it easier for students to grasp social studies concepts, theories, facts, opinions, questions, research, and ideas. They also help sequence events as outlined in the content standards.

. . . result in student-made study guides that are compiled as students listen for main ideas, read for main ideas, or conduct research.

. . . provide a multitude of creative formats in which students can present projects, research, interviews, and inquiry-based reports instead of the typical poster board or social studies fair formats.

. . . replace teacher-generated writing or photocopied sheets with student-generated print.

. . . incorporate the use of such skills as comparing and contrasting, recognizing cause and effect, and finding similarities and differences into daily work and long-term projects. For example, these Foldables can be used to compare and contrast student explanations and/or opinions currently accepted by experts in the field of social studies.

. . . continue to "immerse" students in previously learned vocabulary and concepts, information, primary and secondary source data, surveys, and more.

. . . can be used by students or teachers to easily communicate data through graphs, tables, charts, models, and diagrams, including Venn diagrams.

. . . allow students to make their own journals for recording observations, research information, primary and secondary source data, surveys, and more.

. . . can be used as alternative assessment tools by teachers to evaluate student progress or by students to evaluate their own progress.

. . . integrate language arts, the sciences, and math into the study of social studies.

. . . provide a sense of student ownership in the social studies curriculum.

National Social Studies Standards and Communication Skills

The National Social Studies Standards stress the importance of communication skills in social studies education. Not all students will become government officials, geographers, or historians, but all students need to be able to think, analyze, and communicate using social studies skills. Throughout their lives, students will be called upon to be social studies literate as they make observations, analyze and recall empirical data, read and differentiate between fact and opinion, discuss pros and cons of actions and reactions, justify voting for or against an issue, research a topic related to their well being or interests, make cause-and-effect decisions about their actions, write editorials to express their views publicly, and more. Foldables are one of many techniques that can be used to integrate reading, writing, thinking, debating, researching, and other communication skills into an interdisciplinary social studies curriculum.

Foldable Basics

What to Write and Where

Teach students to write general information--titles, vocabulary words, concepts, questions, main ideas, and dates--on the front tabs of their Foldables. General information is viewed every time a student looks at a Foldable. Foldables help students focus on and remember key points without being distracted by other print.

Ask students to write specific information—supporting ideas, student thoughts, answers to questions, research information, empirical data, class notes, observations, and definitions—under the tabs.

As you teach, demonstrate different ways in which Foldables can be used. Soon you will find that students make their own Foldables and use them independently for study guides and projects.

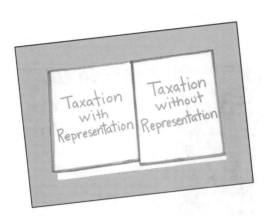

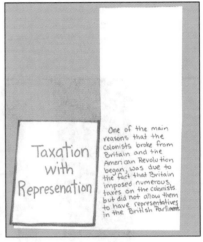

With or Without Tabs

Foldables with flaps or tabs create study guides that students can use to self check what they know about the general information on the front of tabs. Use Foldables without tabs for assessment purposes (where it's too late to self check) or projects where information is presented for others to view quickly.

Venn Diagram used as a study guide

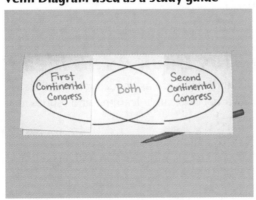

Venn Diagram used for assessment

What to Do with Scissors and Glue

If it is difficult for your students to keep glue and scissors at their desks or to carry it from class to class, set up a small table in the classroom and provide several containers of glue, numerous pairs of scissors (sometimes tied to the table), containers of crayons or colored pencils, a stapler, clear tape, and anything else you think students might need to make their Foldables. Don't be surprised if students donate colored markers, decorative-edged scissors, gel pens, stencils, and other art items to your publishing table.

The more they make and use graphic organizers, the faster students become at producing them.

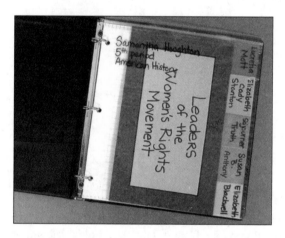

Storing Graphic Organizers in Student Portfolios

Turn one-gallon freezer bags into student portfolios which can be collected and stored in the classroom. Students can also carry their portfolios in their notebooks if they place strips of two-inch clear tape along one side and punch three holes through the taped edge.

Have each student write his or her name along the top of the plastic portfolio with a permanent marker and cover the writing with two-inch clear tape to keep it from wearing off.

Cut the bottom corners off the bag so it won't hold air and will stack and store easily.

> **HINT**: *I found it more convenient to keep student portfolios in my classroom so student work was always available when needed and not "left at home" or "in the car." Giant laundry-soap boxes make good storage containers for portfolios.*

Let Students Use This Book As an Idea Reference

Make this book of lists available to students to use as an idea reference for projects, discussions, social studies debates, extra credit work, cooperative learning group presentations, and more.

Selecting the Appropriate Foldable

Dividing History Concepts into Parts

Foldables divide information and make it visual. In order to select the appropriate Foldable, decide how many parts you want to divide the information into and then determine which Foldable best illustrates or fits those parts. Foldables that are three-dimensional also make the student interact with the data kinesthetically.

For example, if you are studying the three branches of government, you could choose a Foldable that has three tabs (or sections) on the front tabs write *executive*, *legislative*, and *judicial* and under the tabs, place information and examples of each branch

United States History Concepts Already Divided into Parts					
Parts	Concept	Parts	Concept	Parts	Concept
4	Olmec, Maya, Aztec, Inca	13	Colonies	3	Charter, Proprietary, and Royal Colonies
3	Branches of Government	5	Nations of the Iroquois Confederacy	10	First 10 Amendments
2	Patriots and Loyalists	2	Federalists and Democratic-Republicans	3	Before, During, and After the Civil War
2	Allied and Central Powers	3	Terms of Franklin D. Roosevelt	2	Civil Rights and Equal Rights
3	Vietnam War during Kennedy, Johnson, and Nixon	3	NAFTA- United States, Canada, and Mexico		

United States History Concepts That Can Be Divided into Parts		
Native American Groups	Battles of the Revolutionary War	Important Documents
The Constitution	Local, National, and State Laws	Industrial Revolution
Rise and Fall of Prohibition	Causes and Effects of the Cold War	Prosperity of the 1950's
Equal Rights Movement	The Space Race	Events of the 21st Century

Dividing Skills and Foldables into Parts

Reading, writing, and thinking skills can easily be used with Foldables. The following lists show examples of skills and activities and a selection of Foldables divided into parts. You may want to refer to this page as you select activities from the lists of History topics in the third section of this book (see pages 46–83)

Skills and Activities Divided into Parts	
1 Part	**2 Parts**
Find the Main Idea	Compare and Contrast
Predict an Outcome	Cause and Effect
Narrative Writing	Similarities and Differences
Descriptive Writing	Pros and Cons
Expository Writing	Facts and Opinions
Persuasive Writing	Form and Function
3 Parts	**4 Parts**
Venn Diagrams	Who, What, When, Where
Know?-Like to Know?-Learned?	What, Where, When, Why/How
Beginning, Middle, End	
Any Number of Parts	
Questioning	Making and Using Tables
Flow Charts	Making and Using Graphs
Vocabulary Words	Making and Using Charts
Time Lines	Sequencing Data or Events
Concept Webs or Maps	

Foldables Divided into Parts	
1 Part	**2 Parts**
Half Book	Two-Tab Book
Folded Book	Pocket Book
Three-Quarter Book	Shutterfold
Picture-Frame Book	Matchbook Cut in Half
Bound Book	Forward-Backward Book
Matchbook	Concept Map with Two Tabs
3 Parts	**4 Parts**
Trifold Book	Four-Tab Book
Three-Tab Book	Standing Cube
Pyramid Book	Top-Tab Book
Three Pocket Book	Four-Door Book
Concept Map with Three Tabs	
Any Number of Parts	
Accordion Book	Circle Graph
Layered-Look Book	Concept-Map Book
Sentence-Strip Holder	Vocabulary Book
Sentence Strips	Pyramid Mobile
Bound Book	Pop-Up Book
Top-Tab Book (three or more sheets of paper)	Multiple-Pocket Books
Billboard Project	Project Board with Tabs
Display Case	Folded Table, Chart, or Graph

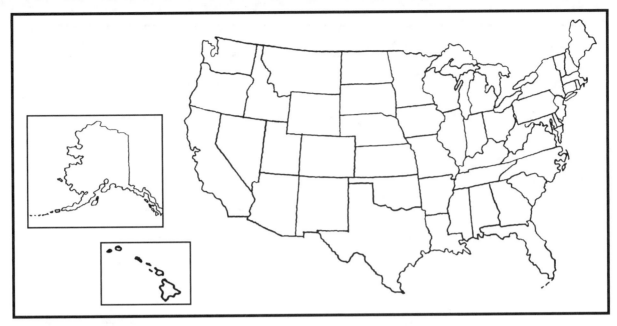

Generic Timeline

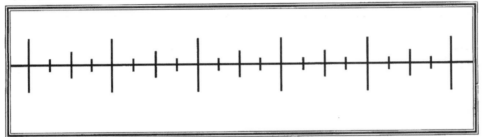

Picture Frame

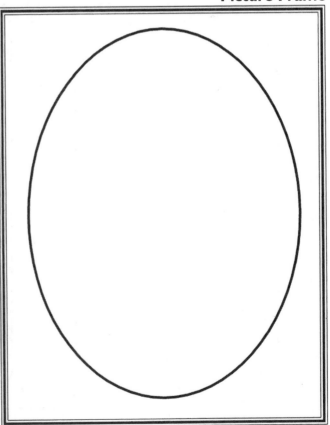

Hundreds Grid

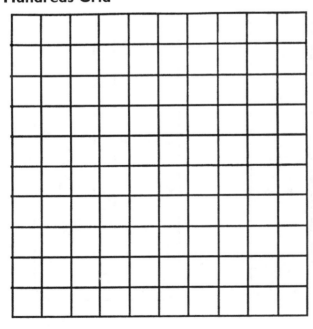

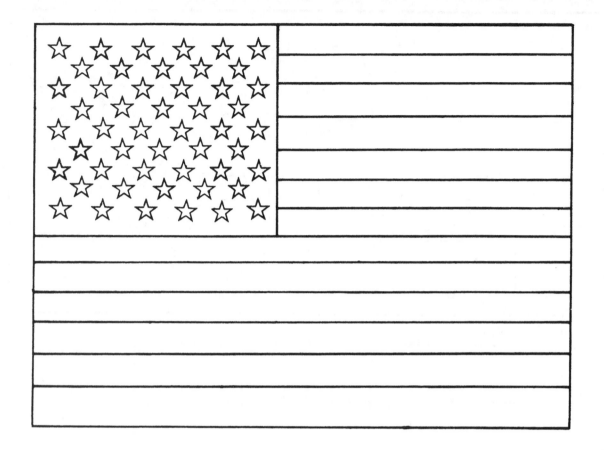

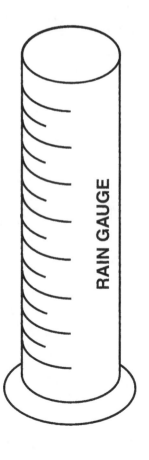

RAIN GAUGE

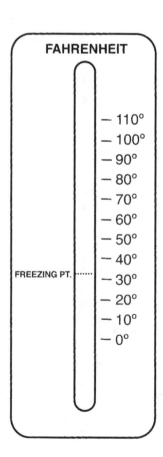

FAHRENHEIT

— 110°
— 100°
— 90°
— 80°
— 70°
— 60°
— 50°
— 40°
FREEZING PT. ······· — 30°
— 20°
— 10°
— 0°

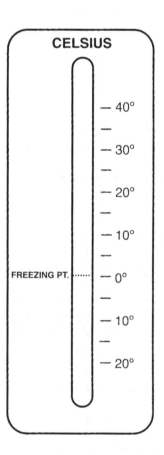

CELSIUS

— 40°
—
— 30°
—
— 20°
—
— 10°
—
FREEZING PT. ······· — 0°
—
— 10°
—
— 20°

Basic Foldable Shapes

The following figures illustrate the basic folds that are referred to throughout the following section of this book

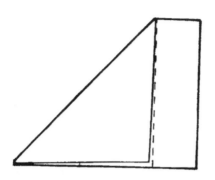

Taco Fold

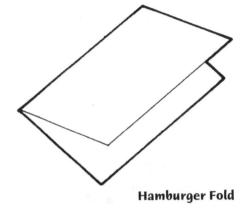

Hamburger Fold

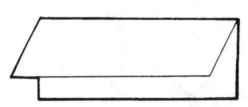

Hot Dog Fold

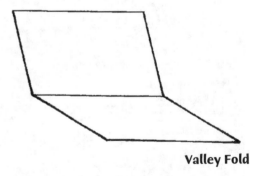

Burrito Fold

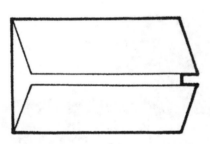

Shutter Fold

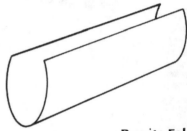

Valley Fold

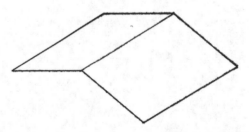

Mountain Fold

Half-Book

Fold a sheet of paper (8 1/2" χ 11") in half.

1. This book can be folded vertically like a *hot dog* or . . .

2. . . . it can be folded horizontally like a *hamburger.*

Use this book for descriptive, expository, persuasive, or narrative writing, as well as graphs, diagrams, or charts.

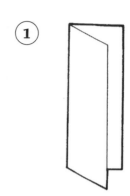

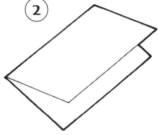

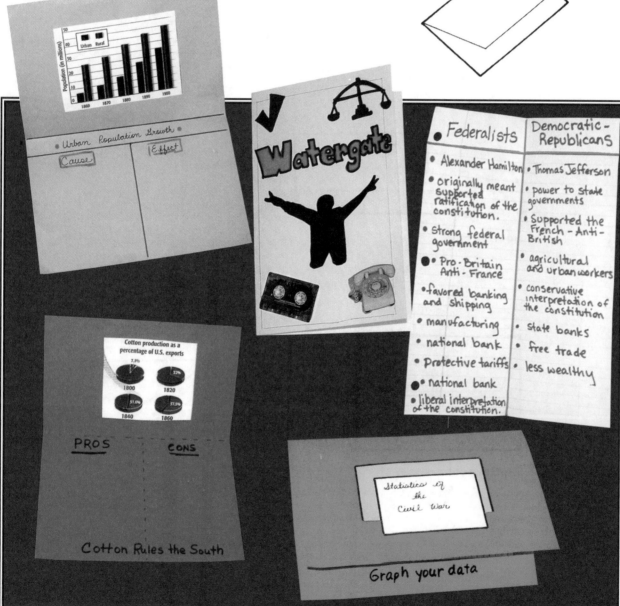

Folded Book

1. Make a *half-book*.

2. Fold it in half again like a *hamburger*. This makes a ready-made cover, and two small pages for information on the inside.

Use photocopied work sheets, Internet print outs, and student-drawn diagrams or maps to make this book. One sheet of paper becomes two activities and two grades.

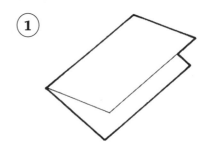

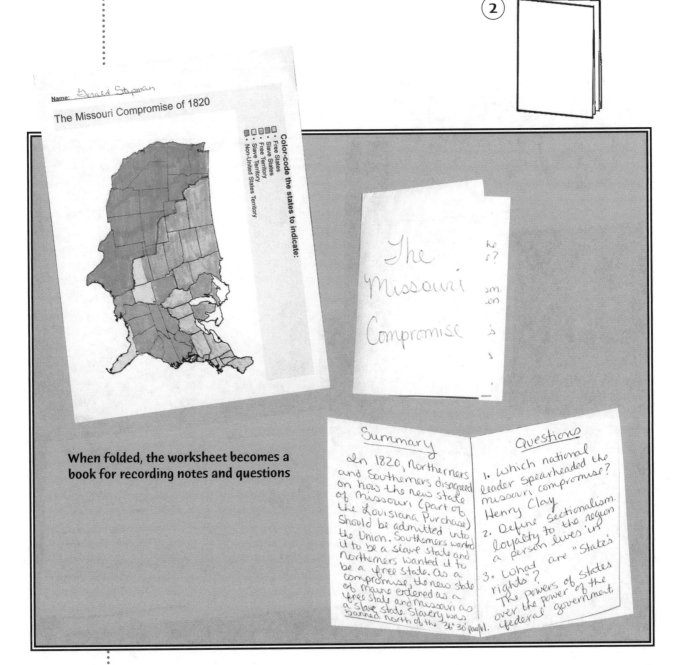

When folded, the worksheet becomes a book for recording notes and questions

Three-Quarter Book

1. Take a *two-tab* book and raise the left-hand tab.

2. Cut the tab off at the top fold line.

3. A larger book of information can be made by gluing several *three-quarter books* side-by-side.

Sketch or glue a graphic to the left, write one or more questions on the right, and record answers and information under the right tab.

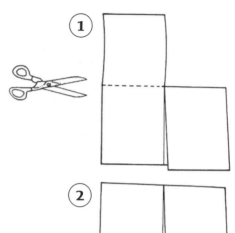

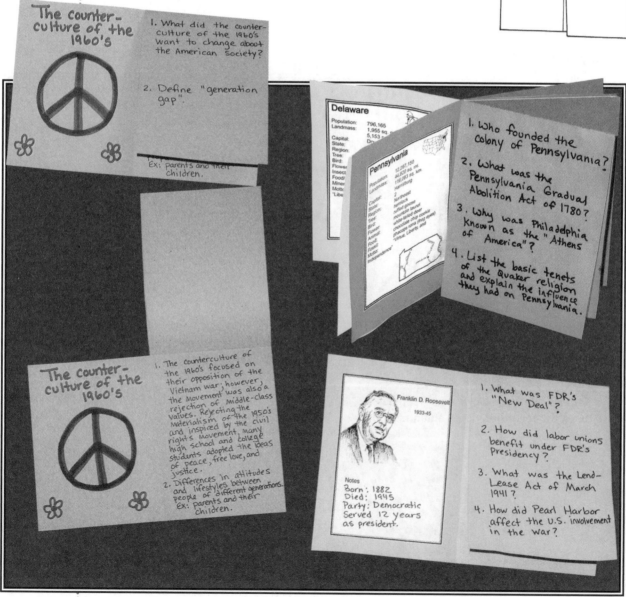

Bound Book

1. Take two sheets of paper (8 1/2" χ 11") and separately fold them like a *hamburger*. Place the papers on top of each other, leaving one sixteenth of an inch between the *mountain tops*.

2. Mark both folds one inch from the outer edges.

3. On one of the folded sheets, cut from the top and bottom edge to the marked spot on both sides.

4. On the second folded sheet, start at one of the marked spots and cut the fold between the two marks.

5. Take the cut sheet from step 3 and fold it like a *burrito*. Place the *burrito* through the other sheet and then open the *burrito*. Fold the bound pages in half to form an eight-page book.

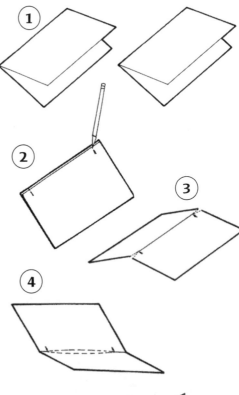

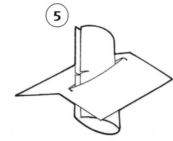

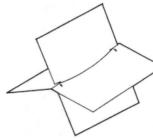

Picture-Frame Book

1. Fold a sheet of paper (8 1/2" χ 11") in half like a *hamburger*.

2. Open the *hamburger* and gently roll one side of the *hamburger* toward the *valley*. Try not to crease the roll.

3. Cut a rectangle out of the middle of the rolled side of the paper leaving a half-inch border, forming a frame.

4. Fold another sheet of paper (8 1/2" χ 11") in half like a *hamburger.* Apply glue to the inside border of the picture frame and place the folded, uncut sheet of paper inside.

Use this book to feature a person, place, or thing. Inside the picture frames, glue photographs, magazine pictures, computer-generated graphs, or have students sketch pictures. This book has three inside pages for writing and recording notes.

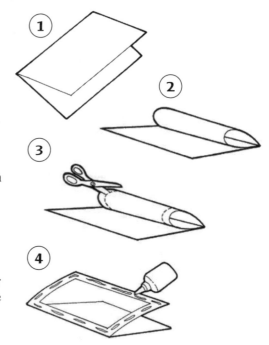

Two-Tab Book

1. Take a *folded book* and cut up the *valley* of the inside fold toward the *mountain top*. This cut forms two large tabs that can be used front and back for writing and illustrations.

2. The book can be expanded by making several of these folds and gluing them side-by-side.

Use this book with data occurring in twos. For example, use it for comparing and contrasting, determining cause and effect, finding similarities and differences, and more.

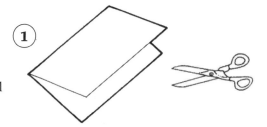

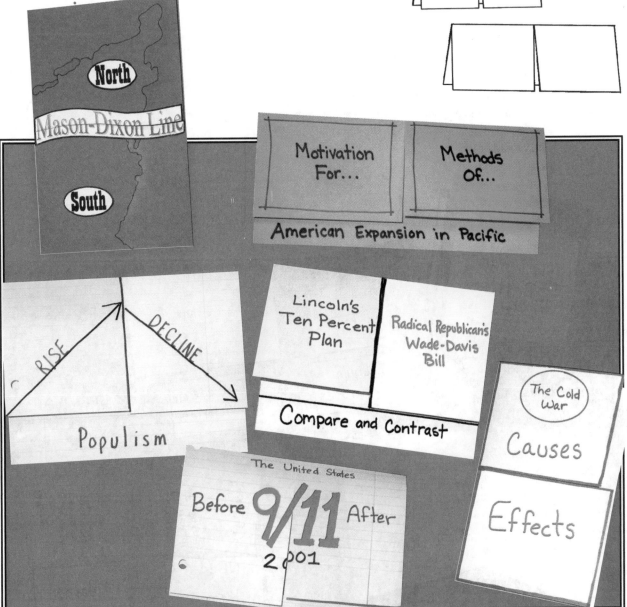

Pocket Book

1. Fold a sheet of paper (8 1/2" χ 11") in half like a *hamburger.*

2. Open the folded paper and fold one of the long sides up two inches to form a pocket. Refold along the *hamburger* fold so that the newly formed pockets are on the inside.

3. Glue the outer edges of the two-inch fold with a small amount of glue.

4. **Optional:** Glue a cover around the *pocket book.*

   Variation: Make a multi-paged booklet by gluing several pockets side-by-side. Glue a cover around the multi-paged *pocket book.*

Use 3" χ 5" index cards and quarter-sheets of notebook paper inside the pockets. Store student-made books, such as two-tab books and folded books in the pockets.

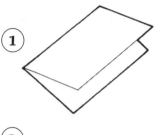

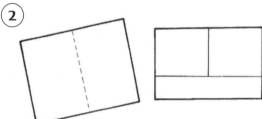

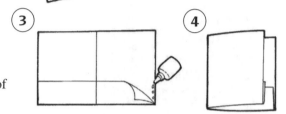

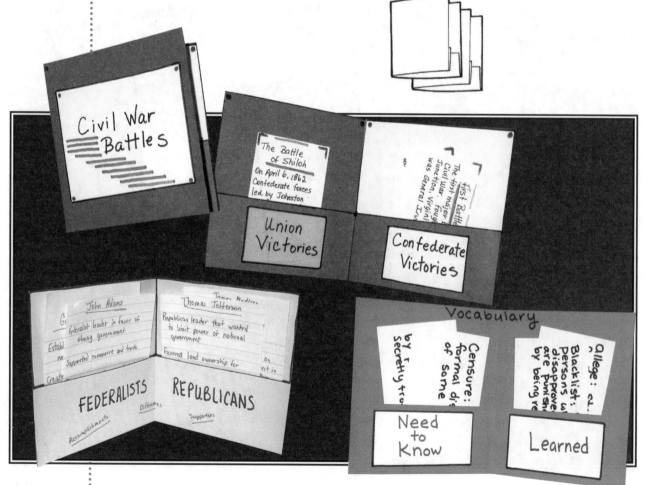

Matchbook

1. Fold a sheet of paper (8 1/2" χ 11") like a *hamburger,* but fold it so that one side is one inch longer than the other side.

2. Fold the one-inch tab over the short side forming an envelope-like fold.

3. Cut the front flap in half toward the *mountain top* to create two flaps.

Use this book to report on one thing, such as one person, place, or thing, or for reporting on two things, such as the cause and effect of the Cold War.

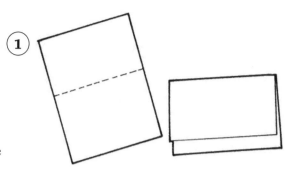

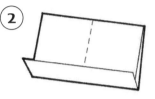

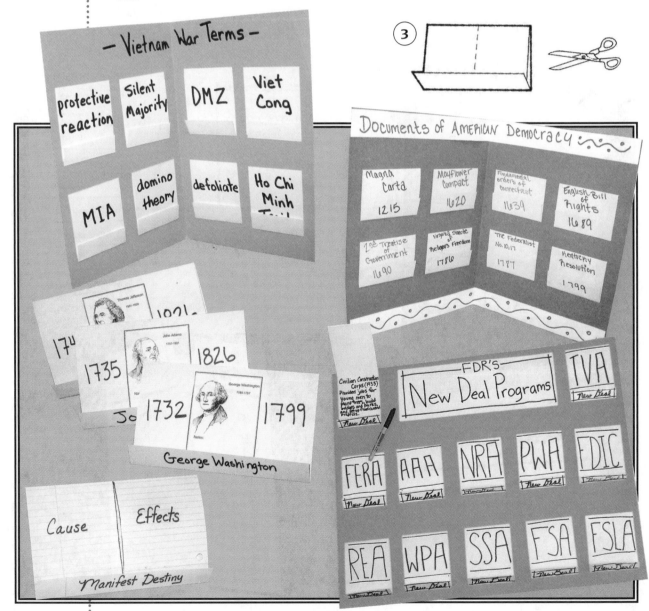

Shutter Fold

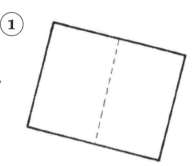

1. Begin as if you were going to make a *hamburger* but instead of creasing the paper, pinch it to show the midpoint.

2. Fold the outer edges of the paper to meet at the pinch, or mid-point, forming a *shutter fold.*

Use this book for data occurring in twos. Or, make this fold using 11" χ 17" paper and smaller books—such as the half book, journal, and two-tab book—that can be glued inside to create a large project full of student work.

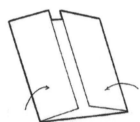

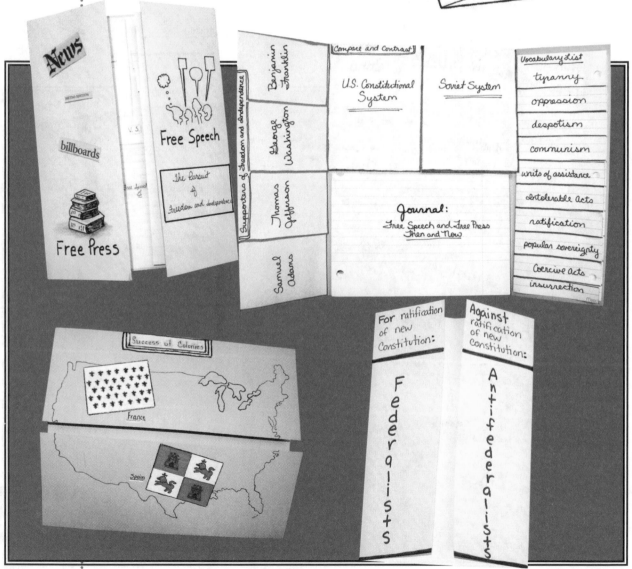

Forward-Backward Book

1. Stack three or more sheets of paper. On the top sheet trace a large circle.

2. With the papers still stacked, cut out the circles.

3. Staple the paper circles together along the left-hand side to create a book.

4. Label the cover and takes notes on the pages that open to the right.

5. Turn the book upside down and label the back. Takes notes on the pages that open to the right.

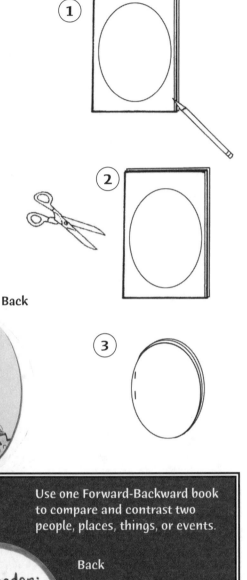

Front

Back

Use one Forward-Backward book to compare and contrast two people, places, things, or events.

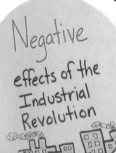

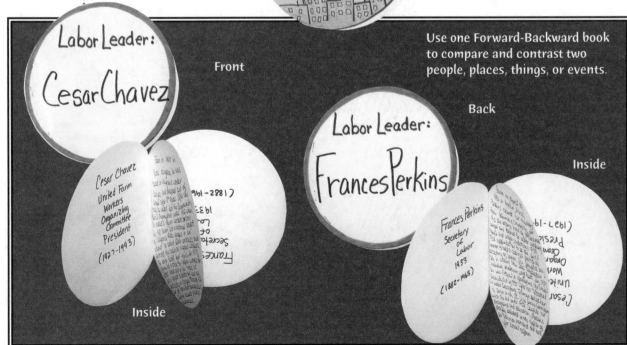

Three-Tab Book

1. Fold a sheet of paper like a *hot dog*.

2. With the paper horizontal, and the fold of the *hot dog* up, fold the right side toward the center, trying to cover one half of the paper.

   NOTE: *If you fold the right edge over first, the final graphic organizer will open and close like a book.*

3. Fold the left side over the right side to make a book with three folds.

4. Open the folded book. Place your hands between the two thicknesses of paper and cut up the two *valleys* on one side only. This will form three tabs.

Use this book for data occurring in threes, and for two-part Venn diagrams.

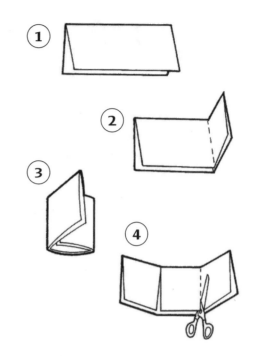

Three-Tab Book Variations

VARIATION A:
Draw overlapping circles on the three tabs to make a Venn Diagram

VARIATION B:
Cut each of the three tabs in half to make a six-tab book.

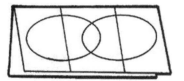

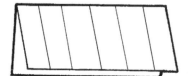

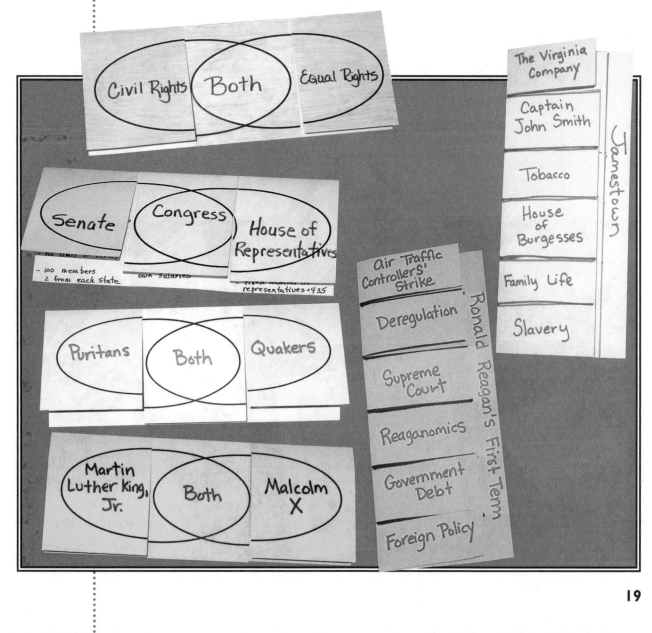

Pyramid Fold

1. Fold a sheet of paper (8 1/2" χ 11") into a *taco*, forming a square. Cut off the excess rectangular tab formed by the fold.

2. Open the folded *taco* and refold it the opposite way forming another *taco* and an X-fold pattern.

3. Cut one of the folds to the center of the X, or the midpoint, and stop. This forms two triangular-shaped flaps.

4. Glue one of the flaps under the other, forming a *pyramid*.

5. Label front sections and write information, notes, thoughts, and questions inside the pyramid on the back of the appropriate tab.

Use to make mobiles and dioramas.
Use with data occurring in threes.

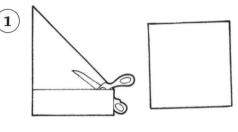

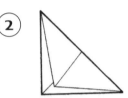

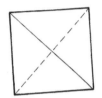

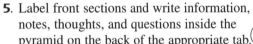

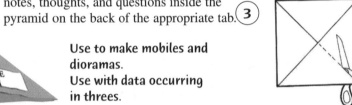

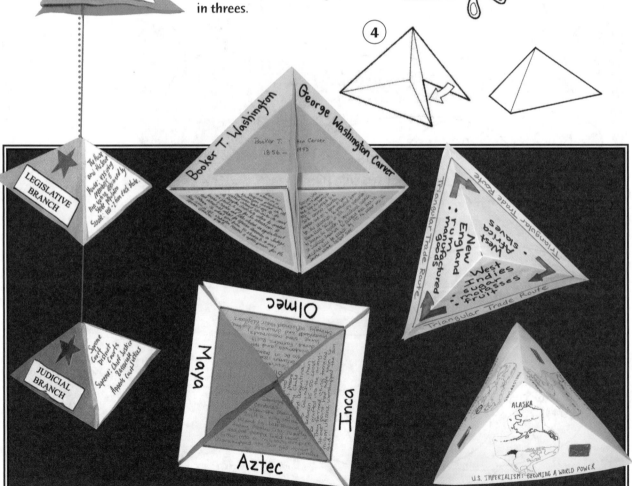

Trifold Book

1. Fold a sheet of paper (8 1/2" χ 11") into thirds.

2. Use this book as is, or cut into shapes. If the trifold is cut, leave plenty of fold on both sides of the designed shape, so the book will open and close in three sections.

Use this book to make charts with three columns or rows, large Venn diagrams, reports on data occurring in threes, or to show the outside and inside of something and to write about it.

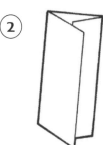

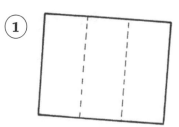

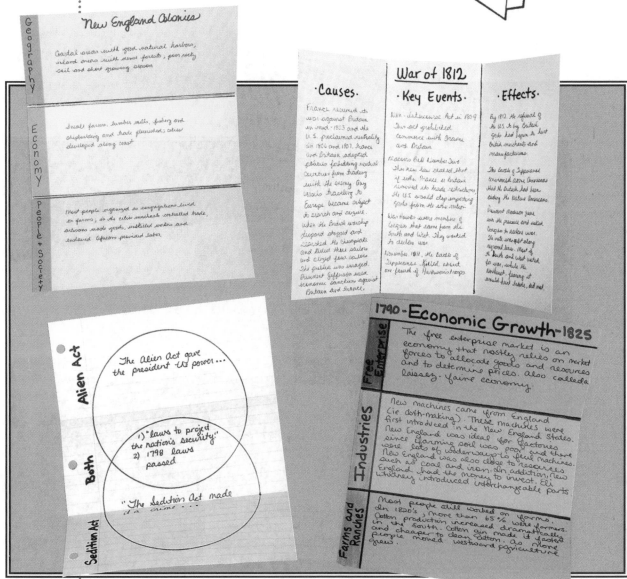

Three Pocket Book

1. Fold a horizontal sheet of paper (11" χ 17") into thirds.

2. Fold the bottom edge up two inches and crease well. Glue the outer edges of the two inch tab to create three pockets.

3. Label each pocket. Use to hold notes taken on index cards or quarter sheets of paper.

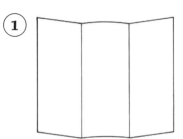

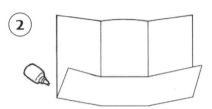

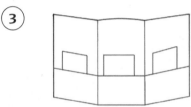

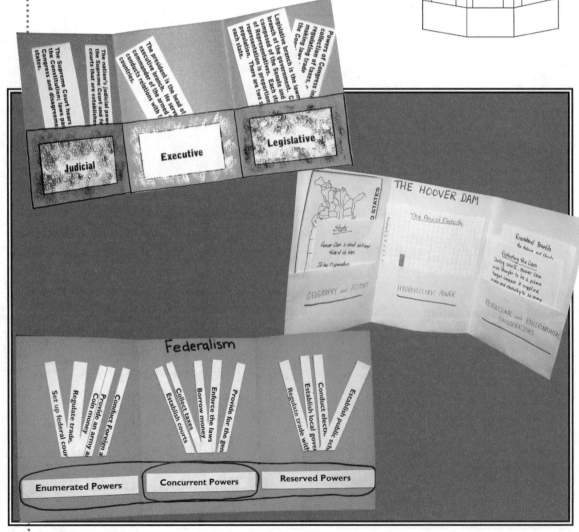

Four-Tab Book

1. Fold a sheet of paper (8 1/2" χ 11") in half like a *hot dog*.

2. Fold this long rectangle in half like a *hamburger*.

3. Fold both ends back to touch the *mountain top* or fold it like an *accordion*.

4. On the side with two *valleys* and one *mountain top*, make vertical cuts through one thickness of paper, forming four tabs.

Use this book for data occurring in fours. For example: who, what, where, when

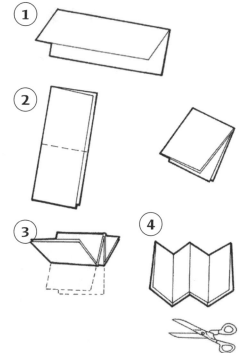

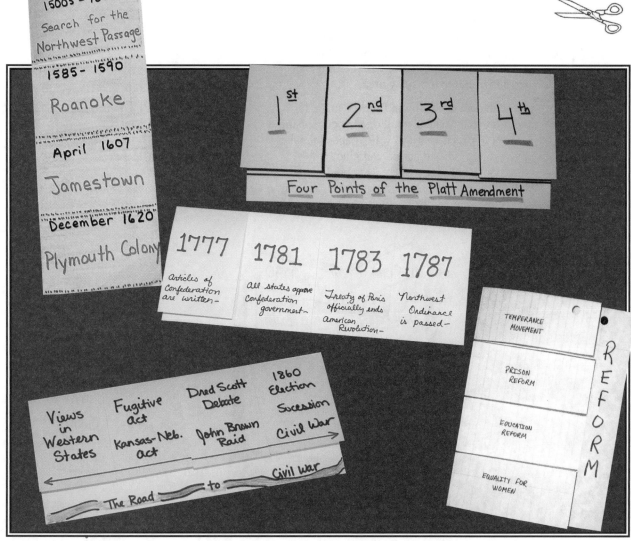

Standing Cube

①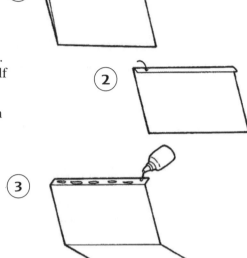

1. Use two sheets of the same size paper. Fold each like a *hamburger*. However, fold one side one half inch shorter than the other side. This will make a tab that extends out one half inch on one side.

2. Fold the long side over the short side of both sheets of paper, making tabs.

3. On one of the folded papers, place a small amount of glue along the the small folded tab, next to the *valley* but not in it.

4. Place the non-folded edge of the second sheet of paper square into the *valley* and fold the glue-covered tab over this sheet of paper. Press flat until the glue holds. Repeat with the other side.

5. Allow the glue to dry completely before continuing. After the glue has dried, the cube can be collapsed flat to allow students to work at their desks. The cube can also be folded into fourths for easier storage, or for moving it to a display area.

Use with data occurring in fours or make it into a project. Make a small display cube using 8 1/2" χ 11" paper. Use 11" χ 17" paper to make large project cubes that you can glue other books onto for display. Notebook paper, photocopied sheets, magazine pictures, and current events also can be displayed on the large cube.

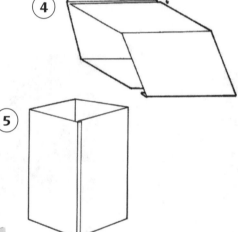

This large cube project can be folded and stored in plastic bag portfolios.

Four-Door Book

1. Make a *shutter fold* using 11" χ 17" or 12" χ 18" paper.

2. Fold the *shutter fold* in half like a *hamburger*. Crease well.

3. Open the project and cut along the two inside *valley* folds.

4. These cuts will form four doors on the inside of the project.

Use this fold for data occurring in fours. When folded in half like a *hamburger*, a finished *four-door book* can be glued inside a large (11" χ 17") *shutter fold* as part of a larger project.

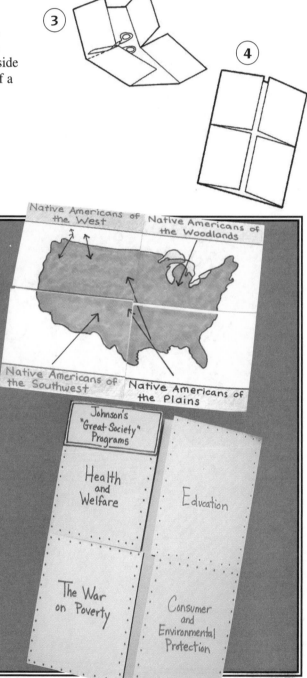

Envelope Fold

1. Fold a sheet of paper (8 1/2" χ 11") into a taco forming a square. Cut off the excess paper strip formed by the square.

2. Open the folded taco and refold it the opposite way forming another taco and an X fold pattern.

3. Open the taco fold and fold the corners toward the center point of the X forming a small square.

4. Trace this square on another sheet of paper. Cut and glue it to the inside of the envelope. Pictures can be placed under or on top of the tabs, or can be used to teach fractional parts.

Use this book for data occurring in fours. For example: North, South, East, and West

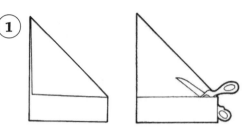

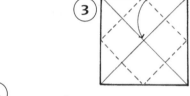

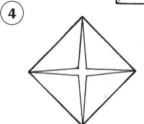

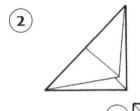

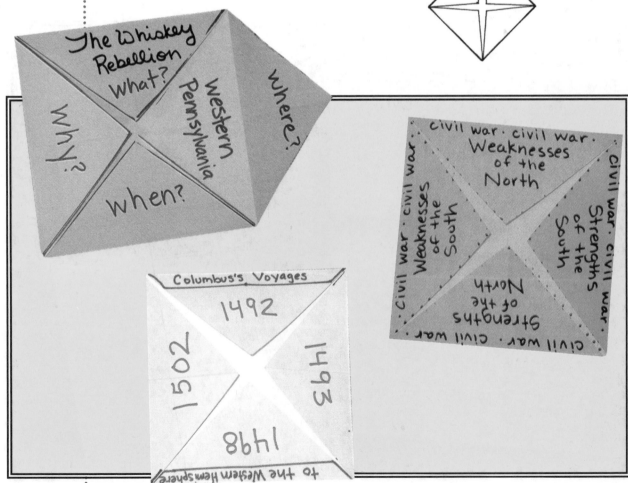

Layered-Look Book

1. Stack two sheets of paper (8 1/2" χ 11") so that the back sheet is one inch higher than the front sheet.

2. Bring the bottom of both sheets upward and align the edges so that all of the layers or tabs are the same distance apart.

3. When all tabs are an equal distance apart, fold the papers and crease well.

4. Open the papers and glue them together along the *valley* or inner center fold or, staple them along the mountain.

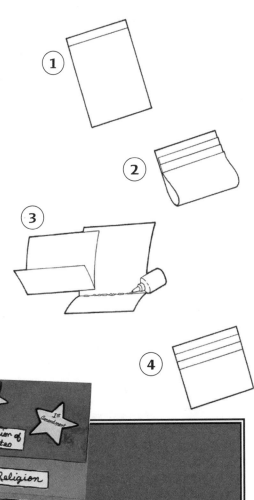

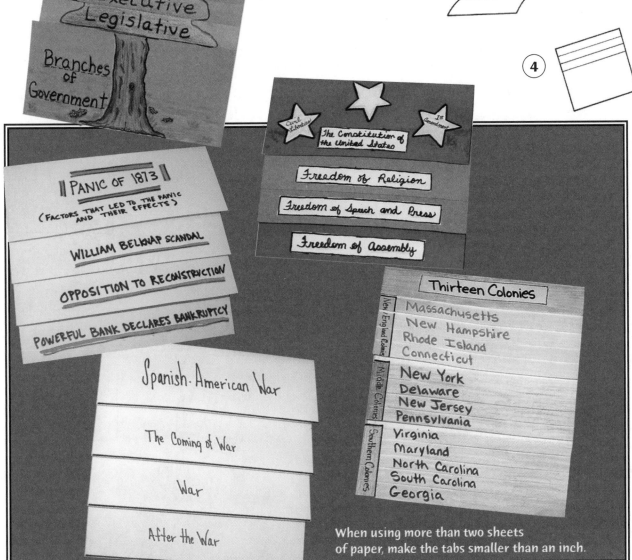

Judicial
Executive
Legislative

Branches
of
Government

Civil Liberties
The Constitution of the United States
1st Amendment

Freedom of Religion

Freedom of Speech and Press

Freedom of Assembly

‖ PANIC OF 1873 ‖

(FACTORS THAT LED TO THE PANIC AND THEIR EFFECTS)

WILLIAM BELKNAP SCANDAL

OPPOSITION TO RECONSTRUCTION

POWERFUL BANK DECLARES BANKRUPTCY

Thirteen Colonies

New England Colonies
Massachusetts
New Hampshire
Rhode Island
Connecticut

Middle Colonies
New York
Delaware
New Jersey
Pennsylvania

Southern Colonies
Virginia
Maryland
North Carolina
South Carolina
Georgia

Spanish-American War

The Coming of War

War

After the War

When using more than two sheets of paper, make the tabs smaller than an inch.

27

Top-Tab Book

1. Fold a sheet of paper (8 1/2" χ 11") in half like a *hamburger.* Cut the center fold, forming two half sheets.

2. Fold one of the half sheets four times. Begin by folding in half like a *hamburger,* fold again like a *hamburger,* and finally again like a *hamburger.* This folding has formed your pattern of four rows and four columns, or 16 small squares.

3. Fold two sheets of paper (8 1/2" χ 11") in half like a *hamburger.* Cut the center folds, forming four half sheets.

4. Hold the pattern vertically and place on a half sheet of paper under the pattern. Cut the bottom right hand square out of both sheets. Set this first page aside.

5. Take a second half sheet of paper and place it under the pattern. Cut the first and second right hand squares out of both sheets. Place the second page on top of the first page.

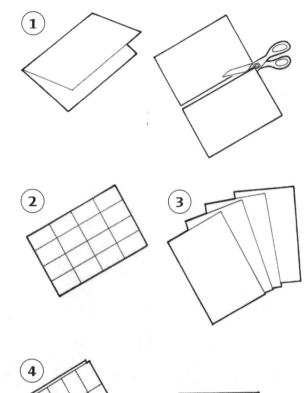

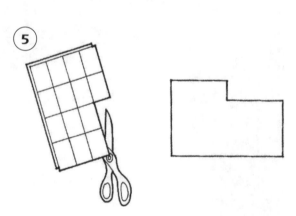

6. Take a third half sheet of paper and place it under the pattern. Cut the first, second, and third right hand squares out of both sheets. Place this third page on top of the second page.

7. Place the fourth, uncut half sheet of paper behind the three cut out sheets, leaving four aligned tabs across the top of the book. Staple several times on the left side. You can also place glue along the left paper edges, and stack them together. The glued spine is very strong.

8. Cut a final half sheet of paper with no tabs and staple along the left side to form a cover.

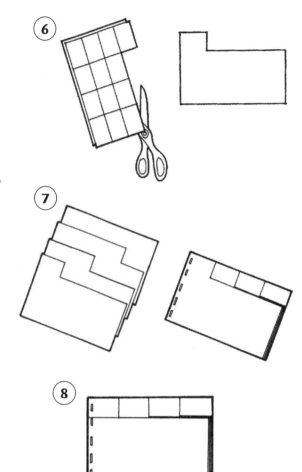

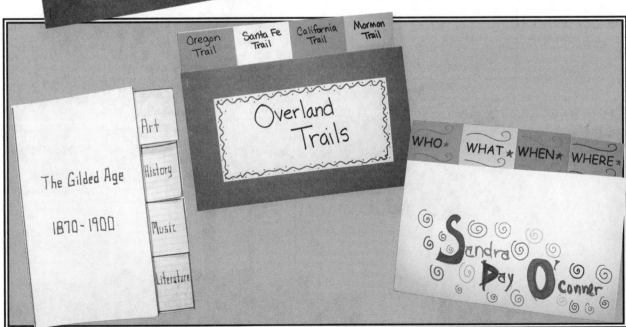

Accordion Book

NOTE: *Steps 1 and 2 should be done only if paper is too large to begin with.*

1. Fold the selected paper into *hamburgers*.

2. Cut the paper in half along the fold lines.

3. Fold each section of paper into *hamburgers*. However, fold one side one half inch shorter than the other side. This will form a tab that is one half inch long.

4. Fold this tab forward over the shorter side, and then fold it back away from the shorter piece of paper (in other words, fold it the opposite way).

5. Glue together to form an *accordion* by gluing a straight edge of one section into the *valley* of another section.

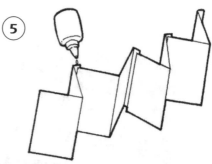

NOTE: *Stand the sections on end to form an accordion to help students visualize how to glue them together. (See illustration.)*

Always place the extra tab at the back of the book so you can add more pages later.

Use this book for timelines, student projects that grow, sequencing events or data, and biographies.

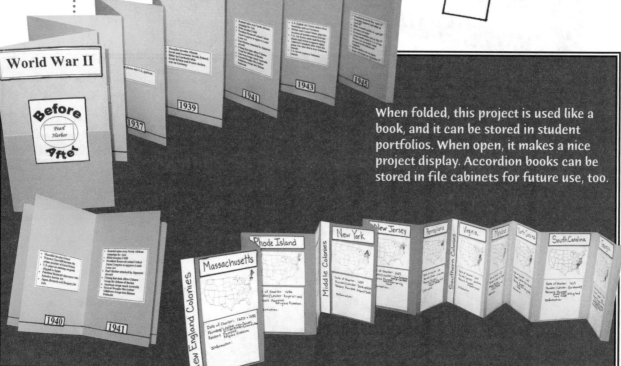

When folded, this project is used like a book, and it can be stored in student portfolios. When open, it makes a nice project display. Accordion books can be stored in file cabinets for future use, too.

Pop-Up Book

1. Fold a sheet of paper (8 1/2" χ 11") in half like a *hamburger.*

2. Beginning at the fold, or *mountain* top, cut one or more tabs.

3. Fold the tabs back and forth several times until there is a good fold line formed.

4. Partially open the *hamburger* fold and push the tabs through to the inside.

5. With one small dot of glue, glue figures for the *pop-up book* to the front of each tab. Allow the glue to dry before going on to the next step.

6. Make a cover for the book by folding another sheet of paper in half like a *hamburger.* Place glue around the outside edges of the *pop-up book* and firmly press inside the *hamburger* cover.

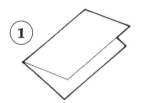
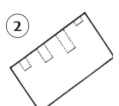
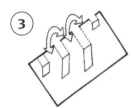
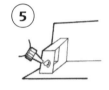
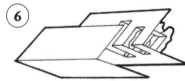
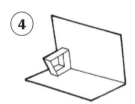

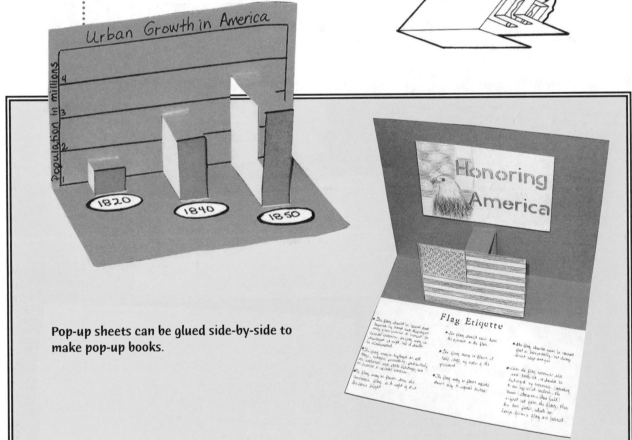

Pop-up sheets can be glued side-by-side to make pop-up books.

Folding into Fifths

1. Fold a sheet of paper in half like a hotdog or hamburger for a five tab book, or leave open for a folded table or chart.

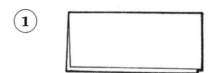

2. Fold the paper so that one third is exposed and two thirds are covered.

3. Fold the two thirds section in half.

4. Fold the one third section (single thickness) backward to form a fold line.

The paper will be divided into fifths when opened

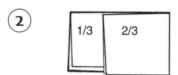

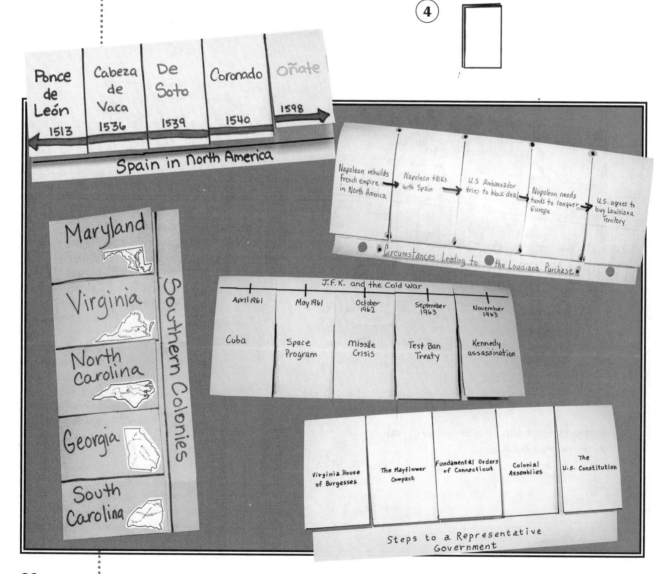

Folded Table or Chart

1. Fold the number of vertical columns needed to make the table or chart.

2. Fold the horizontal rows needed to make the table or chart.

3. Label the rows and columns.

Remember: Tables are organized along vertical and horizontal axes, while charts are organized along one axis, either horizontal or vertical.

Table

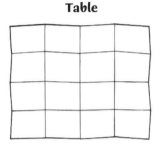

Chart

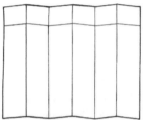

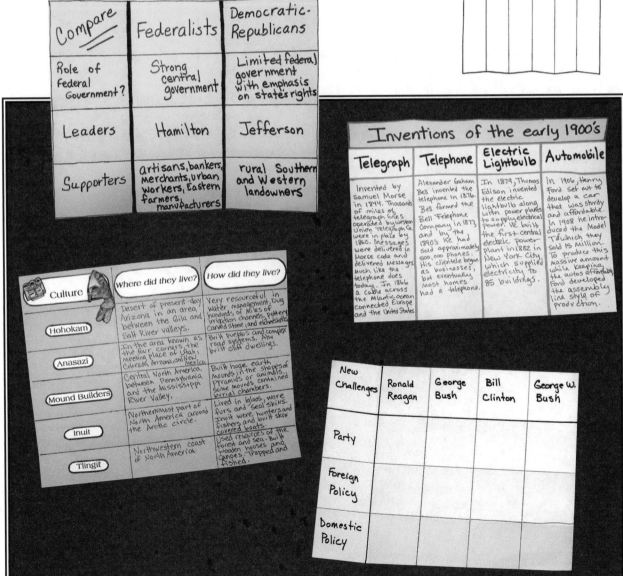

Compare	Federalists	Democratic-Republicans
Role of federal Government?	Strong central government	Limited federal government with emphasis on states rights
Leaders	Hamilton	Jefferson
Supporters	artisans, bankers, merchants, urban workers, Eastern farmers, manufacturers	rural Southern and Western landowners

Inventions of the early 1900's

Telegraph	Telephone	Electric Lightbulb	Automobile
Invented by Samuel Morse in 1844. Thousands of miles of telegraph lines operated by Western Union Telegraph Co. were in place by 1860. Messages were delivered in Morse code and delivered messages today, like the telephone does today. In 1866 a cable across the Atlantic ocean connected Europe and the United States	Alexander Graham Bell invented the telephone in 1876. Bell formed the Bell Telephone Company in 1877, and by the 1890's he had sold approximately 500,000 phones. His clientele began as businesses, but eventually most homes had a telephone.	In 1879, Thomas Edison invented the electric lightbulb along with power plants to supply electrical power. He built the first central electric power plant in 1882 in New York City, which supplied electricity to 85 buildings.	In 1906, Henry Ford set out to develop a car that was sturdy and affordable. In 1908 he introduced the Model T which they sold 15 Million. To produce this massive amount while keeping the autos affordable Ford developed the assembly line style of production.

Culture	Where did they live?	How did they live?
Hohokam	Desert of present-day Arizona in an area between the Gila and Salt River valleys.	Very resourceful in water management. Dug hundreds of miles of irrigation channels. Pottery carved stone and etched shells
Anasazi	In the area known as the four corners, the meeting place of Utah, Colorado, Arizona, and New Mexico.	Built Pueblos and complex road systems. Also built cliff dwellings.
Mound Builders	Central North America between Pennsylvania and the Mississippi River Valley.	Built huge earth mounds in the shapes of pyramids or animals. Some mounds contained burial chambers.
Inuit	Northernmost part of North America around the Arctic circle.	Lived in igloos, wore furs and seal skins. Inuit were hunters and fishers and built skin covered boats.
Tlingit	Northwestern coast of North America.	Used resources of the forest and sea. Built wooden houses and canoes. Trapped and fished.

New Challenges	Ronald Reagan	George Bush	Bill Clinton	George W. Bush
Party				
Foreign Policy				
Domestic Policy				

Folding a Circle into Tenths

1. Fold a paper circle in half.

2. Fold the half circle so that one third is exposed and two thirds are covered.

3. Fold the one third (single thickness) backward to form a fold line.

4. Fold the two thirds section in half.

5. The half circle will be divided into fifths. When opened, the circle will be divided into tenths.

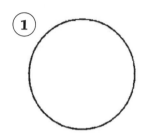

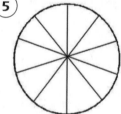

NOTE: *Paper squares and rectangles are folded into tenths the same way. Fold them so that one third is exposed and two thirds is covered. Continue with steps 3 and 4.*

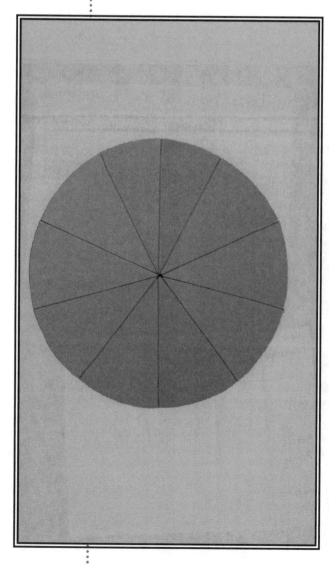

Circle Graph

1. Cut out two circles using a pattern.

2. Fold one of the circles in half on each axis, forming fourths. Cut along one of the fold lines (the radius) to the middle of each circle. Flatten the circle.

3. Slip the two circles together along the cuts until they overlap completely.

4. Spin one of the circles while holding the other stationary. Estimate how much of each of the two (or you can add more) circles should be exposed to illustrate given percentages or fractional parts of data. Add circles to represent more than two percentages.

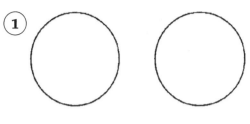

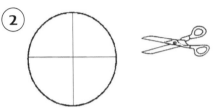

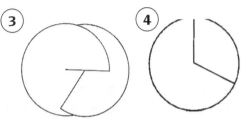

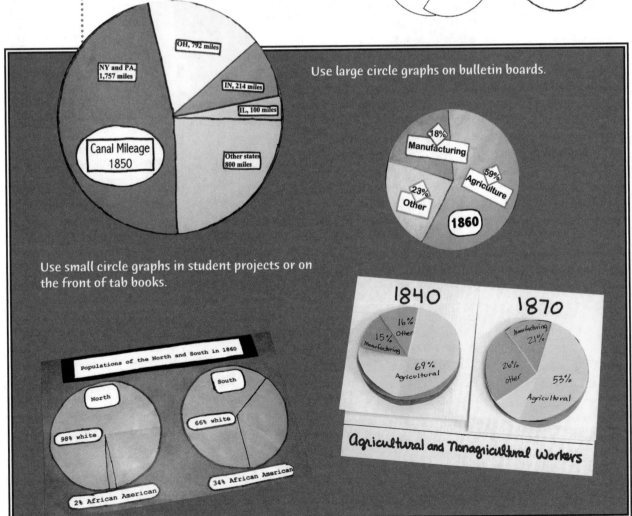

Use large circle graphs on bulletin boards.

Use small circle graphs in student projects or on the front of tab books.

OH, 792 miles

NY and PA, 1,757 miles

IN, 214 miles

IL, 100 miles

Canal Mileage 1850

Other states 800 miles

18% Manufacturing

59% Agriculture

23% Other

1860

Populations of the North and South in 1860

North

98% white

2% African American

South

66% white

34% African American

1840

16% Other

15% Manufacturing

69% Agricultural

1870

Manufacturing 21%

26% other

53% Agricultural

Agricultural and Nonagricultural Workers

Vocabulary Book

1. Fold a sheet of notebook paper in half like a *hotdog*.

2. On one side, cut every third line. This results in ten tabs on wide ruled notebook paper and twelve tabs on college ruled.

3. Label the tabs.

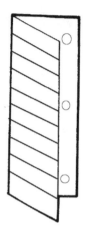
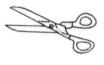

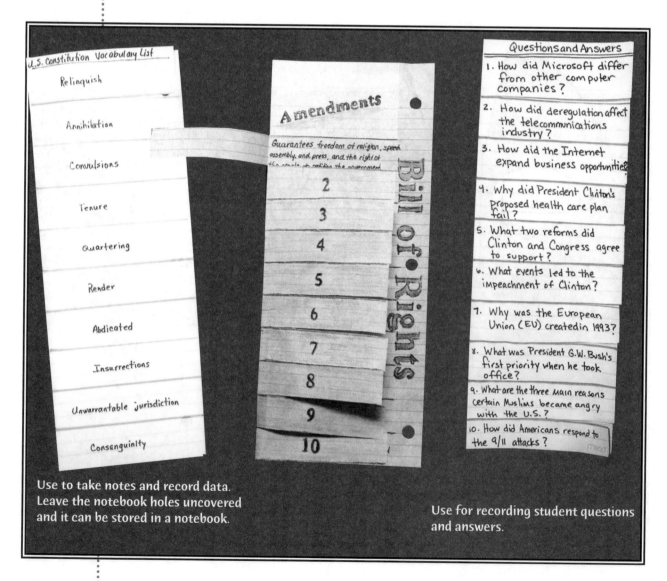

U.S. Constitution Vocabulary List

Relinquish

Annihilation

Convulsions

Tenure

Quartering

Render

Abdicated

Insurrections

Unwarrantable jurisdiction

Consanguinity

Amendments

Guarantees freedom of religion, speech, assembly, and press, and the right of the people to petition the government

2
3
4
5
6
7
8
9
10

Bill of Rights

Questions and Answers

1. How did Microsoft differ from other computer companies?

2. How did deregulation affect the telecommunications industry?

3. How did the Internet expand business opportunities?

4. Why did President Clinton's proposed health care plan fail?

5. What two reforms did Clinton and Congress agree to support?

6. What events led to the impeachment of Clinton?

7. Why was the European Union (EU) created in 1993?

8. What was President G.W. Bush's first priority when he took office?

9. What are the three main reasons certain Muslims became angry with the U.S.?

10. How did Americans respond to the 9/11 attacks?

Use to take notes and record data. Leave the notebook holes uncovered and it can be stored in a notebook.

Use for recording student questions and answers.

Concept-Map Book

1. Fold a sheet of paper along the long or short axis, leaving a two-inch tab uncovered along the top.

2. Fold in half or in thirds.

3. Unfold and cut along the two or three inside fold lines.

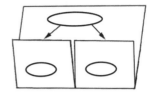

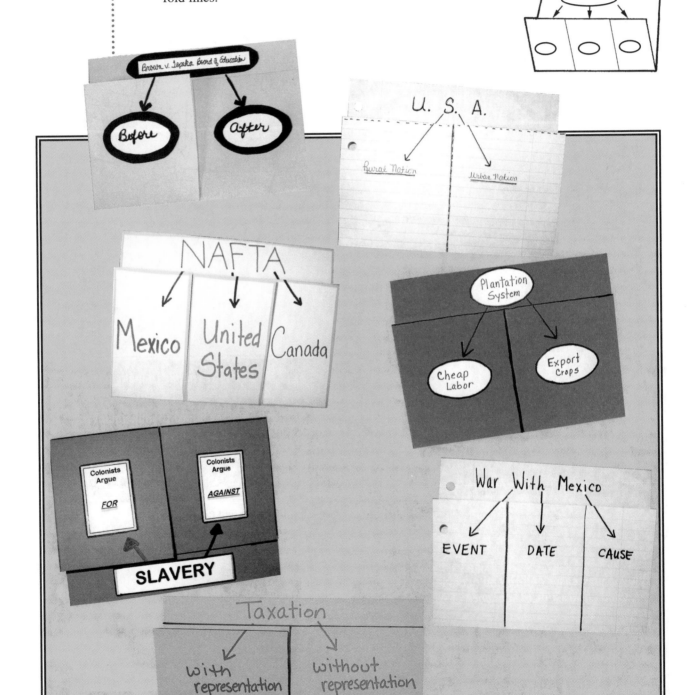

Four-Door Diorama

1. Make a *four-door book* out of a *shutter fold.*

2. Fold the two inside corners back to the outer edges (*mountains*) of the *shutter fold.* This will result in two *tacos* that will make the *four-door book* look like it has a shirt collar. Do the same thing to the bottom of the *four-door book.* When finished, four small triangular *tacos* have been made.

3. Form a 90-degree angle and overlap the folded triangles to make a display case that doesn't use staples or glue. (It can be collapsed for storage.)

4. Or, as illustrated, cut off all four triangles, or *tacos*. Staple or glue the sides.

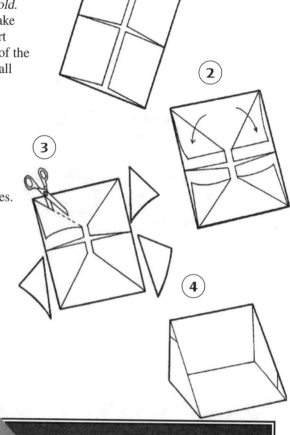

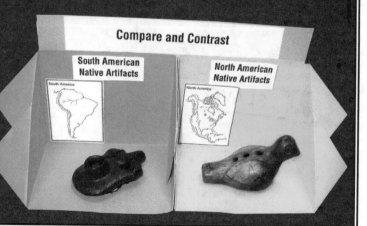

Use 11″ ⅹ 17″ paper to make a large display case.

Use poster board to make giant display cases.

Glue display cases end-to-end to compare and contrast or to sequence events or data.

Display Case

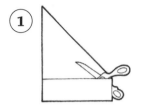

1. Make a *taco* fold and cut off the rectangular tab formed. This will result in a square.

2. Fold the square into a *shutter fold.*

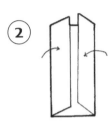

3. Unfold and fold the square into another *shutter fold* perpendicular to the direction of the first. This will form a small square at each of the four corners of the sheet of paper.

4. As illustrated, cut along two fold lines on opposite sides of the large square.

5. Collapse in and glue the cut tabs to form an open box.

How to Make a Lid

Fold another open-sided box using a square of paper one half inch larger than the square used to make the first box. This will make a lid that fits snugly over the display box. *Example:* If the base is made out of an 8 1/2" paper square, then make the top out of a 9" square.

Cut a hole out of the lid and cover the opening with a cut piece of acetate used on overhead projectors. Heavy, clear plastic wrap or scraps from a laminating machine also will work. Secure the clear plastic sheet to the inside of the lid with glue or tape.

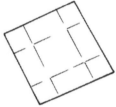

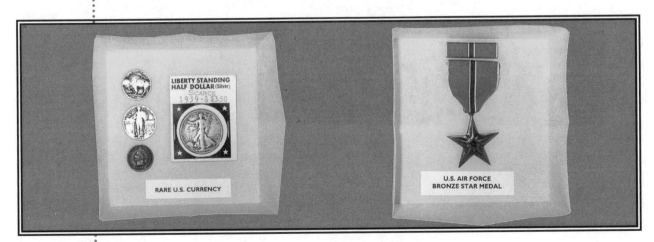

RARE U.S. CURRENCY

U.S. AIR FORCE BRONZE STAR MEDAL

Project Board with Tabs

1. Draw a large illustration or a series of small illustrations or write on the front of one of the pieces of selected-size paper.

2. Pinch and slightly fold the paper at the point where a tab is desired on the illustrated project board. Cut into the paper on the fold. Cut straight in, then cut up to form an "L." When the paper is unfolded, it will form a tab with an illustration on the front.

3. After all tabs have been cut, glue this front sheet onto a second piece of paper. Place glue around all four edges and in the middle, away from tabs.

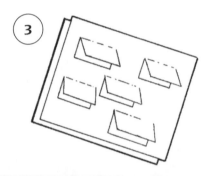

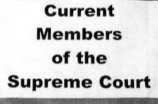

Write or draw under the tabs. If the project is made as a bulletin board using butcher paper, quarter and half-sheets of paper can be glued under the tabs.

Billboard Project

1. Fold all pieces of the same size of paper in half like *hamburgers*.

2. Place a line of glue at the top and bottom of one side of each folded billboard section and glue them edge-to-edge on a background paper or project board. If glued correctly, all doors will open from right to left.

3. Pictures, dates, words, etc., go on the front of each billboard section. When opened, writing or drawings can be seen on the inside left of each section. The base, or the part glued to the background, is perfect for more in-depth information or definitions.

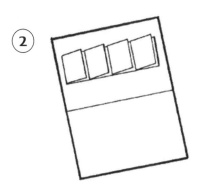

Use for timelines or sequencing data, such as major battles of the Civil War.

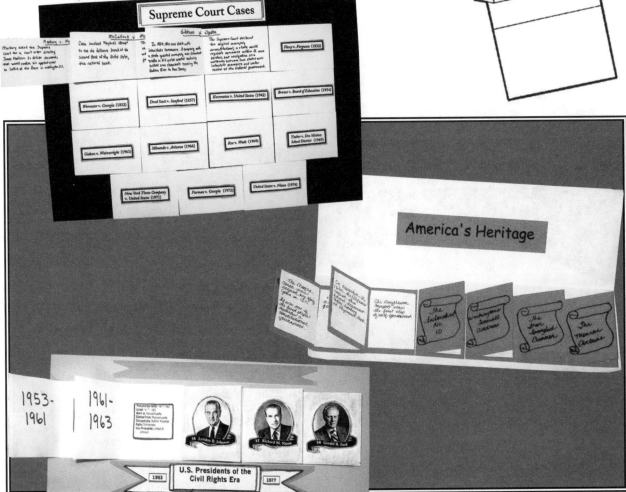

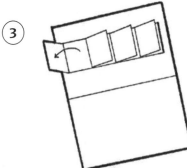

41

Sentence Strips

1. Take two sheets of paper (8 1/2" x 11") and fold into hamburgers. Cut along the fold lines making four half sheets. *(Use as many half sheets as necessary for additional pages to your book.)*

2. Fold each sheet in half like a hotdog.

3. Place the folds side-by-side and staple them together on the left side.

4. 1" from the stapled edge, cut the front page of each folded section up to the mountain top. These cuts form flaps that can be raised and lowered.

To make a half-cover, use a sheet of construction paper one inch longer than the book. Glue the back of the last sheet to the construction paper strip leaving one inch, on the left side, to fold over and cover the original staples. Staple this half-cover in place.

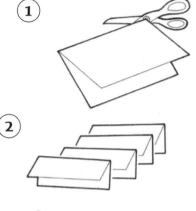

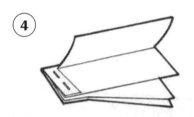

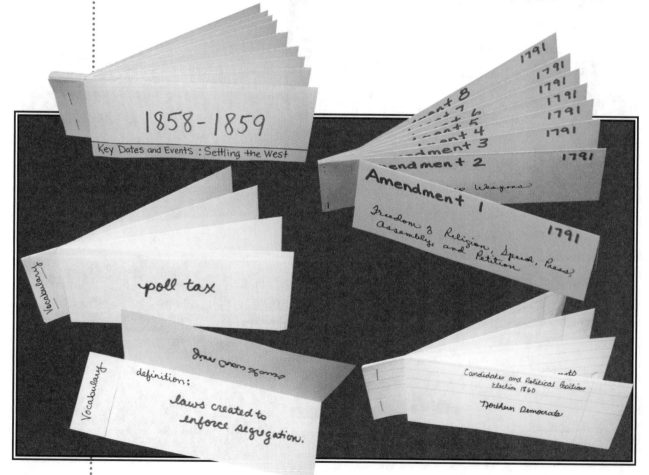

Sentence-Strip Holder

1. Fold a sheet of paper (8 1/2" χ 11") in half like a *hamburger*.

2. Open the *hamburger* and fold the two outer edges toward the *valley*. This forms a *shutter fold*.

3. Fold one of the inside edges of the shutter back to the outside fold. This fold forms a floppy "L."

4. Glue the floppy L-tab down to the base so that it forms a strong, straight L-tab.

5. Glue the other shutter side to the front of this L-tab. This forms a tent that is the backboard for the flashcards or student work to be displayed.

6. Fold the edge of the L-tab up one quarter to one half to form a lip that will keep the student work from slipping off the holder.

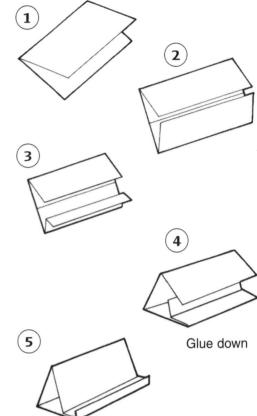

Glue down

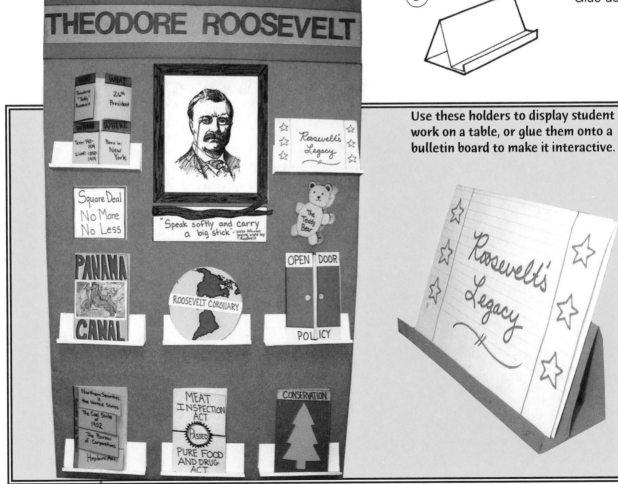

Use these holders to display student work on a table, or glue them onto a bulletin board to make it interactive.

United States History Topic Ideas

General Topics

The following United States History topics are covered in this section.

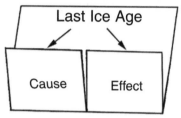

1x2 Chart

Artifacts
Can Tell	Can't Tell

Last Ice Age

Two-tab concept map

Cause → Effect

Compare	Nomadic Culture	Farming Culture
Life		
Society		

3x3 Table

Nomadic Cultures	Farming Cultures

Two-tab book

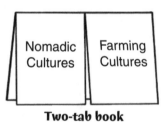

Flora | Fauna

Shutter-fold book

Prehistoric America

Skill	Activity Suggestion	Foldable Parts
K-LK-L	ask yourself what you know, what you would like to know, and review what you learn about Prehistoric America	3
describe	three factors that shaped the Old Stone Age: • an Ice Age which began about 100,000 years ago and ended about 12,000 years ago • development of basic tools • fire used for cooking, light, and as a method for hunting animals	3
research and report on	two different theories as to how the First Americans came to the North American continent	2
	the last Ice Age which ended about 12,000 years ago, and its effect on North America	2
	glaciation and the effects glaciers have had on North America--past and present	2
	carbon dating and its importance to archaeologists and historians	2
differentiate	between paleontology and archaeology	2
search the web	for pictures of and information on the earliest known North American artifacts such as stone tools, weapons, pottery, baskets, wood or stone carvings, more	any number
explain	what can and can not be learned about the culture of early peoples based upon artifacts	2
locate	Beringia and Bering Strait on a map or globe	2
investigate	the popular theory that nomadic people from Asia crossed Beringia into present-day Alaska then present and justify an alternative theory	2
use	locations and dates of artifact discoveries to map the possible migration routes of peoples across the Americas	any number
discover	what the American flora and fauna was like when these first people arrived: • fauna: mastodons, woolly mammoth, saber-toothed tigers, giant bison, others • flora: cedar, oak, willow, hackberry, others	any number
speculate	as to what might have caused the extinction of the giant mammals and describe what changes these extinctions caused in the lives of early people	2
write	a fictional account of how maize might have been discovered and used 9,000 years ago in Mexico	1
compare and contrast	life for prehistoric people before and after they learned to plant maize	2
	nomadic cultures, farming cultures, both	3
learn about	other crops cultivated by early people and explain their importance--past and present • tomatoes • beans • squashes and pumpkins • potatoes	2
research	life and culture of a nomadic society and life and culture of a farming society	2
explain	how different cultures develop	1

Ancient Civilizations of the Americas

Skill	Activity Suggestion	Foldable Parts
K-LK-L	ask yourself what you know, what you would like to know, and review what you learn about ancient civilizations of the Americas	3
make a timeline	for each of the following civilizations: • the Olmec • the Maya • the Aztec • the Inca	4
give examples	of ways in which the Maya, Aztec, and Inca civilizations abused their natural environment to meet their needs	3
	of ways in which each of the three main civilizations changed their natural environment to meet their needs	3
research	who, what, when, and where of the following: • the Olmec • the Maya • the Aztec • the Inca	4
summarize	the rise and decline of an early civilization	2
investigate	what is known about the giant cities that prospered during these civilizations	1
make a table	to show what is known about the following for each of the three civilizations: • agriculture and/or economics • architecture and construction • religion • communication (writing, calendars, oral history) • government	5
determine	how geography influenced the cultural development of each of the following: • the Olmec, coastal lands, Gulf of Mexico • the Maya, rain forests, Central America • the Aztec, lake island of Tenochititlan, Central Mexico • the Inca, sides of the Andes Mountains	4

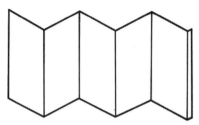

Timeline: Ancient Civilizations

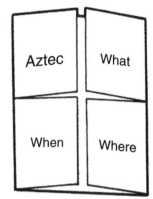

Four-door book

Four-tab book

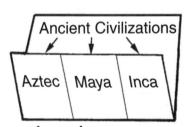

Three-tab concept map

	Ag./ Econ.	Archi.	Religion	Comm.	Gov.
Maya					
Aztec					
Inca					

6x4 Table

Pre-Columbian North Americans

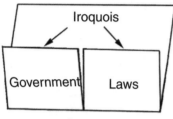

West | **Woodlands**

Southwest | **Plains**

Four-door book

Iroquois

Government | **Laws**

Two-tab concept map

	West	South-west	Woodland	Plains
Flora				
Fauna				
Geology				

5x4 Table

Describe	What	Where
Mesa Verde		
Monk's Mound		
Miami Circle		

3x4 Chart

Skill	Activity Suggestion	Foldable Parts
K-LK-L	ask yourself what you know, what you would like to know, and review what you learn about the Native Americans before the arrival of Columbus	3
research	early Native American tribes living in the following regions: • West • Southwest • Plains • Woodlands	4
	the government and laws of a group of Native American people, such as the Iroquois	2
investigate	the flora, fauna, and geography of each of the four regions and speculate as to how Native Americans met their basic needs of food, shelter, transportation, and clothing in each	4
make a timeline	to sequence what is known about the following cultures: • Hohokam, Southwest • Anasazi, Southwest • Mound Builders, Ohio River valley	any number
speculate	as to the greatest threats to Native American groups before and after the arrival of European explorers	2
make a Venn diagram	describe and compare the following: • the Mound Builders, the Anasazi, both • the Hohokam, the Anasazi, both • the Mound Builders, the Hohokam, both	3
search the web	for information on "what" and "where" of any of the following historic locations and/or artifacts: • Monk's Mound, largest mound in Cahokia • Great Serpent Mound • Pueblo Bonito • Mesa Verde • Miami Circle • Clovis Point	2
write	five journal entries describing a weeks worth of events taking place in the life of an imaginary person living in Pueblo Bonito	5
design and draw	the floor plan of a group of rooms and kivas that form a yet undiscovered pueblo village	1
speculate	as to how giant mounds of earth were made and shaped by the Mound Building cultures	2
	as to why the Hohokam, Anasazi, and Mound Builders cultures disappeared before European explorers	3
compare	the huge geoglyphs in Mississippi and California with the Nazca geoglyphs in Peru	2
list	advantages and disadvantages of cliff dwellings	2
research	the use of irrigation by early Native Americans	1
explain	how archaeologists know that trade took place between early peoples	1

Native Americans

Skill	Activity Suggestion	Foldable Parts
K-LK-L	ask yourself what you know, what you would like to know, and review what you learn about the Native Americans living in America when the explorers arrived	3
outline	two early Native American encounters with Europeans	2
describe	peaceful and warring Native American cultures	2
make a timeline	sequencing the history of a group of Native American people after 1492: • North: Inuit • West: Tlingit, Chinook, NezPerce, Pomo, Ute, Shoshone, • Southwest: Hopi, Zuni, Acoma, Apache, Navajo • Plains: Apache, Dakota • Woodlands: Iroquois, Cherokee, Creek, Chicksaw	any number
compare and contrast	Native American life before and after reservations were established	2
differentiate	between the roles of men and women among different Native American peoples	2
show cause and effect	of a decline in Native American peoples across North America	2
make a table	and use it to collect information on Native Americans of the North, West, Southwest, Plains, and Woodlands: • diet and methods of obtaining food • shelter from elements • clothing • transportation • climate adaptations	5
make a Venn diagram	describe and compare any of the following cultures: • Iroquois, Cherokee, both • Ute, Shoshone, both • Inuit, Tlingit, both • Nez Perce, Hopi, both • Apache, Dakota, both	3
read to discover	two technological developments of Native Americans	2
	three modes of transportation	3
	two or more forms of communication used	2+
	two or more types of currency used	2+
	three or more kinds of architecture	3+
investigate	the who, what, when, where of any of the following people: • Chief Joseph • Quanah Parker • Sitting Bull • Tecumseh • American Horse • Cochise • Joseph • Red Cloud • Standing Bear • Little Wolf • Crazy Horse • Dull Knife • Little Crow	4

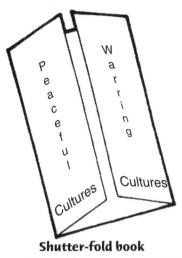

Shutter-fold book

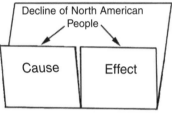

Two-tab concept map

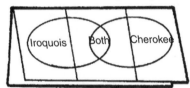

Three-tab Venn diagram

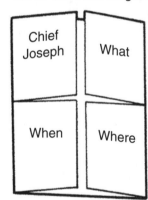

Four-door book

1x2 Chart

Exploring the Americas

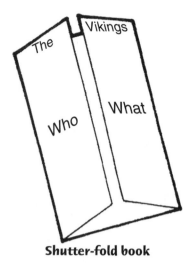

Shutter-fold book

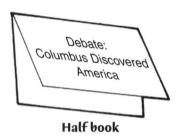

Half book

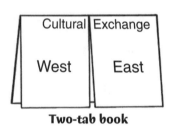

Two-tab book

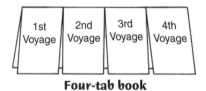

Four-tab book

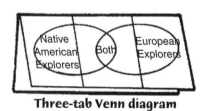

Three-tab Venn diagram

Skill	Activity Suggestion	Foldable Parts
K-L‑K-L	ask yourself what you know, what you would like to know, and review what you learn about exploring America	3
describe	the Vikings and what they discovered as the first Europeans to explore the Western Hemisphere	2
explain	how and why Columbus prepared for his first voyage	2
investigate	the land and the people first seen by Christopher Columbus--Taino people on the island of San Salvador, also called Watling Island	2
debate	the statement "Columbus discovered America."	1
list	three effects of the "discovery" of the Western Hemisphere on the Native Americans and the explorers	3
outline	the chain of events that took place after Columbus met the native people of North America	any number
analyze	the effects of the exchange of cultures between Eastern and Western Hemispheres	2
investigate	the Columbian exchange and list plants and animals native to the Americas taken to Europe and then on to other countries by explorers: • pineapple, tomatoes, corn, chili peppers, avocados, potatoes, pumpkins, turkeys, others	2
	the Columbian exchange and list plants and animals native to Europe brought to the Americas by explorers: • wheat, peaches, cucumbers, oranges, grapes, sugar, horses, cattle, sheep, etc.	2
make a Venn diagram	of Native Americans, first Europeans, both	3
	of Columbus, Amerigo Vespucci, and both	3
compare and contrast	Columbus's four voyages to the Western Hemisphere between 1492 and 1502	4
investigate	two ways in which explorers reported their discoveries to others	2
describe	an explorer's actions and the world's reactions to discoveries made	2
make a table	of information on explorers, discoveries made, and the outcome of the discoveries	3
discover	when your community was first explored by Europeans and describe what they saw	2
explain	how people native to the Americas could have been explorers within the Americas	1
compare and contrast	Native American explorers and European explorers in the Americas	2
	mapmaking, past and present	2
read and report	on the history of mapmaking	any number
speculate	as to what, if anything, is left for explorers to discover and geographers to map in the Americas	1
explain	why the search for a northwest passage was important, who attempted to discover it, and when it was finally accomplished (1906)	3
determine	how the search for a northwest passage led to increased colonization of North America	1

Exploring the Americas: Spain

Skill	Activity Suggestion	Foldable Parts
K-LK-L	ask yourself what you know, what you would like to know, and review what you learn about Spain's exploration of America	3
outline	how conquistadors hoped to obtain wealth for themselves and for their monarchy	2
map and describe	the route Cortes took as he sailed across the Gulf of Mexico and marched across Mexico to Tenochititlan	1
outline	the events that led to the fall of Tenochtitlan	any number
explain	how explorers became conquerors and differentiate between the two	2
compare and contrast	Mexico before and after Hernando Cortes conquered the Aztec people	2
	the conquerors and the conquered	2
make a Venn diagram	Montezuma, Hernando Cortez, and both	3
describe	Dona Marina and explain how she helped Hernando Cortes	2
find	similarities and differences between Spain and New Spain	2
investigate	the who, what, when, where of any of the following people: • Christopher Columbus • Hernando Cortes • Juan Ponce de Leon • Hernando de Soto • Francisco Vasquez de Coronado • Francisco Pizarro • Diego de Almagro • Francisco de Orellana • Amerigo Vespucci • Vicente Yanez Pinzon • Pedro Alvares Cabral • Vasco Nunez de Balboa	4
argue	against the encomienda system	1
show	cause and effect of disease brought by conquerors	2
describe	how the search for gold expanded the lands of New Spain	1
make a timeline	to show the exploration and conquering of North America by the Spanish	any number
	to show the exploration and conquering of South America by the Portuguese	any number
research	the Inca civilization before and after Pizarro defeated Atahualpa and conquered the Incas	2
compare and contrast	the conquering of the Aztec people in Mexico and the conquering of the Inca people in Peru	2
make a timeline	of the history of St. Augustine, Florida, Spain's first settlement in present-day United States	any number
list	four locations of Spanish missions in North America and briefly describe each	4
locate on a map	the territory claimed by Spain in the late 1600's	1
	the El Camino Real and the missions along this road	2
Venn diagram	Spanish California, Spanish Texas, both	2
describe	the three types of settlements allowed by Spanish Law: pueblos, missions, and presidios	3
	how and why plantations were created	2

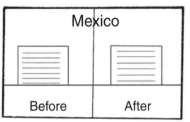

Pocket book

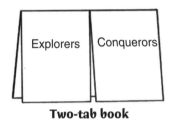

Two-tab book

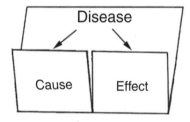

Two-tab concept map

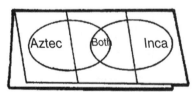

Three-tab Venn diagram

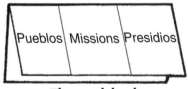

Three-tab book

Exploring the Americas: France

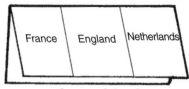

Three-tab book

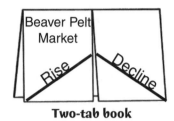

Two-tab book

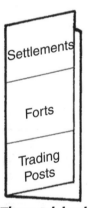

Three-tab Venn diagram

Three-tab book

Journal of a French Fur Trapper

Bound book

Skill	Activity Suggestion	Foldable Parts
K-LK-L	ask yourself what you know, what you would like to know, and review what you learn about the French in North America	3
give	reasons why France, England, and the Netherlands wanted to find a Northwest Passage	3
explain	why France (and countries other than Spain and Portugal) were in violation of the Treaty of Tordesillas when they sent explorers to North America	1
investigate	the who, what, when, where of any of the following: • Jacques Cartier • Henry Hudson • Samuel de Champlain • Louis Joliet and Jacques Marquette	4
describe	the importance of French exploration of and claims to the territory around the Mississippi River, called Louisiana, after King Louis XIV	2
locate on a map	the territory claimed by France in the late 1600s and describe the land past and present	2
explain	how fishing and the fur trade brought wealth and power to France	2
research	the rise and decline of a market for beaver pelts and explain why it occurred	2
compare and contrast	French and Spanish relations with Native Americans	2
	New Spain and New France	2
make a timeline	of the development of at least four French colonies and trading posts that became large cities: • Quebec • St. Louis • Detroit • Chicago	4
determine	how French settlements, forts, and trading posts prohibited the expansion of English colonies	3
	the relationship between the French and the Native Americans	2
	the relationship between the French and the Dutch who were also establishing trading posts in the north east	2
investigate	the who, what, when, and where of one of the following: • Robert La Salle • King Henry IV of France • Samuel de Champlain • Jacques Marguette • Louis Jolliet • Jean Baptiste Point du Sable	4
write	five imaginary journal entries made by a French fur trapper bringing furs to a trading post	5
research	the immigration to America in the late 1600's of the Huguenots, French Protestants: • why did they come? • how many came? • where did they settle?	3

English Settlements and Colonies

Skill	Activity Suggestion	Foldable Parts
K-LK-L	ask yourself what you know, what you would like to know, and review what you learn about the first settlements and colonies in America	3
investigate	England's first (1585) and second (1587) attempts to start colonies in America	2
show	cause and effect of the war between Spain and England and the colonization of America	2
determine	how groups of people seeking religious freedom influenced the development of the thirteen colonies: Pilgrims, Puritans, Quakers, and Catholics	4
make a Venn diagram	of Puritans, Pilgrims, both	3
research	the Powhatan people, Chief Powhatan, and his daughter Pocahontas	3
outline	the key events in the establishment of one of the following: • Jamestown Colony, 1607 • Plymouth Colony, 1620 • Williamsburg, 1633	any number
investigate	the celebration of Thanksgiving held by the Pilgrims and the Wampanoag people in 1621	1
	the what, where, when, and why/how of the "Lost Colony" of Roanoke Island, 1587	4
locate and describe	the New England, Middle, and Southern colonies	3
outline	the history of the development of the New England Colonies, Middle Colonies, and Southern Colonies	3
make a timeline	that shows the establishment, development, and growth of all thirteen colonies	any number
locate	the New England Colonies on a map: • Connecticut, Massachusetts, New Hampshire, Rhode Island	4
	the four Middle Colonies on a map: • New Jersey, New York, Pennsylvania, Delaware	4
	the five Southern Colonies on a map: • Maryland, Virginia, North Carolina, Georgia, South Carolina	5
make a table	of information on the thirteen colonies: • founder, reason for founding, location, economy, natural resources, historic events, first settlers	any number
make a Venn diagram	indentured servants, slaves, both	3
	New England colonies, Middle Colonies, both	3
	Middle Colonies, Southern Colonies, both	3
	New England Colonies, Southern Colonies, both	3
outline	the history of slavery in the English colonies	any number
investigate	the who, what, when, where of any of the following: • William Penn • John Winthrop • William Penn • James Oglethorpe • Lord Baltimore • Metacomet, Wampanoag leader	4

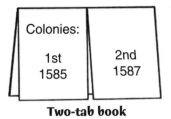

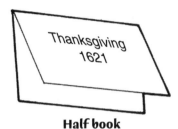

Two-tab book

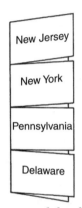

Half book

Four-tab book

Three-tab Venn diagram

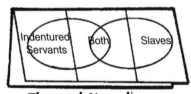

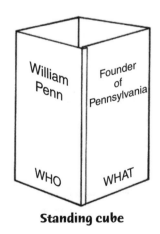

Standing cube

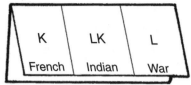

Three-tab book

Three-tab book

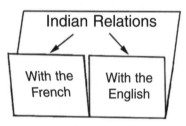

Two-tab concept map

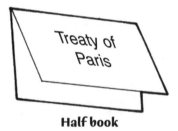

Half book

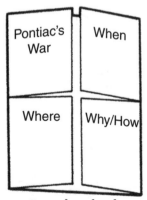

Four-door book

The French and Indian War

Skill	Activity Suggestion	Foldable Parts
K-LK-L	ask yourself what you know, what you would like to know, and review what you learn about the French and Indian War	3
outline	the long history of events that led to a serious rivalry between the French and English before the 1740's	any number
	the history of events from 1740 to 1754 that increased the rivalry and animosity between the nations	any number
give	two reasons the French did not want the British along the Ohio River valley and north	2
explain	how the French and Indian War got its name, when it started, and why	3
	who led the Virginia militia to the Ohio Valley to stop the French from building a fort on British territory, and why did the colonists get involved in this action	2
describe	actions taken by the English colonies before, during, and after the war	3
outline	the major events of the French and Indian War 1754-1763	any number
compare and contrast	Indian relations with the French and the British	2
	Iroquois relations with the French and the British	2
mark	the boundaries of the British colonies before and after the French and Indian War	2
list	three resources that helped the British win the war	3
summarize	the terms of the Treaty of Paris (1763)	1
discuss	the positions of France, England, and Spain at the end of the French and Indian War	3
investigate	Pontiac's Rebellion (1763)	1
research	the who, what, when, and where of one of the following: • George Washington • William Pitt • General Edward Braddock • Jeffrey Amherst and James Wolfe • General Amherst • General Louis Joseph Montcalm • Chief Pontiac	4
	the what, where, when, why/how of the following: • Seven Year's War, 1756 • Treaty of Paris, 1763 • Pontiac's War, 1763 • Proclamation of 1763	4
search the web	for information on some of the important forts that played a part in the war and describe if they exist today: • Fort Necessity • Fort Duquesne • Fort Fontenac • Fort Louisbourg • Fort Ticonderoga • Fort Oswego • Fort William Henry, others	any number

Unrest in the Colonies

Skill	Activity Suggestion	Foldable Parts
K-LK-L	ask yourself what you know, what you would like to know, and review what you learn about unrest in the American colonies	3
discover	two ways in which the French and Indian war contributed to unrest in the colonies: • British war debt resulted in harsh tax policies and the colonists were angry because they were being taxed without representation • Royal Proclamation of 1763 restricted colonial expansion west of the Appalachian Mountains	2
describe	British actions and colonial reactions that contributed to the revolution	2
research	what, when, where, why/how of one of the following: • the Sons of Liberty • the Boston Tea Party • the Stamp Act Congress	4
	who, what, when, where of one of the following: • Daughters of Liberty • Michael Johnson (also called Crispus Attucks)	4
make a Venn diagram	of the Stamp Act, Townshend Acts, and both	3
	of the First Continental Congress, Second Continental Congress, both	3
make a timeline	to sequence British actions that led to unrest: • Royal Proclamation of 1763 • customs reform and duties • American Revenue Act, 1764, also called the Sugar Act • Currency Act of 1764 • Stamp Act, 1765 • Quartering Act, 1765 • Declaratory Act, 1766 • Townshend Acts, 1767 • Revenue Act of 1767 (part of the Townshend Act) • legalization of writs of assistance, or search warrants • 1,000 British troops sent to Boston to maintain order • Boston Massacre, 1770 • Townshend Acts repealed, but tax on tea remained • Tea Act, 1773 • Coercive Acts, 1774 • Quebec Act, 1774 • Intolerable Acts: both Quebec Act and Coercive Acts	any number
report on	two major Colonial reactions that led to war: • burning of the customs ship, Gaspee • Boston Tea Party	2

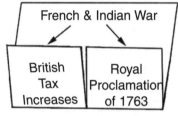

1x2 Chart

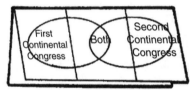

Two-tab concept map

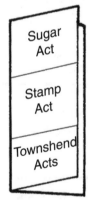

Three-tab Venn diagram

Three-tab book

Shutter-fold book

The American Revolution

Bound book

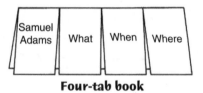

Two-tab book

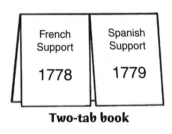

Four-tab book

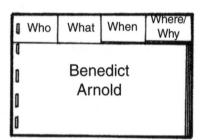

Top-tab book

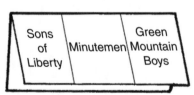

Three-tab book

Skill	Activity Suggestion	Foldable Parts
K-LK-L	ask yourself what you know, what you would like to know, and review what you learn about the American Revolution	3
compare and contrast	colonial self-government and the government of England	2
show causes and effects	of the first two battles of the American Revolution-- Lexington and Concord	2
make a Venn diagram	of battles on land, battles on sea, both	3
sequence and research	five battles of the American Revolution: • Battle of Lexington • Battle of Concord • Battle of Bunker Hill • Battle of Trenton • Battle of Saratoga • Battle of Brandywine Creek • Battle of Kings Mountain • Battle of Yorktown, others	5
write	7 journal entries that might have been made over the period of a week by one of the special trainer minutemen	7
investigate	three authors of the Declaration of Independence: • Thomas Jefferson, John Adams, Benjamin Franklin, Roger Sherman, Robert Livingston, others	3
differentiate	between patriots, loyalists, neutrals	3
list	strengths and weaknesses of the British and Continental armies	2
explain	why the French decided to support the colonists in 1778 and the Spanish in 1779	2
research	the Battle of Yorktown (1781) and the conditions of the Treaty of Paris (1783)	2
make a timeline	of key events of the American Revolution, 1775-1783	any number
investigate	the who, what, when, where of one of the following: • Patrick Henry • Samuel Adams • Abigail Adams • Henry Knox • Paul Revere and William Dawes • George Rogers Clark • John Paul Jones • Francis Marion, "Swamp Fox" • General Charles Cornwallis • Benedict Arnold	4
explain	the purpose of each of the following groups: • Sons of Liberty • Minutemen • Green Mountain Boys	3
compare	the accomplishments of: • the First Continental Congress, 1774 • the Second Continental Congress, 1775	2
list	four factors that contributed to American victory and independence	4

The Constitution

Skill	Activity Suggestion	Foldable Parts
K-LK-L	ask yourself what you know, what you would like to know, and review what you learn about the Constitution of the United States of America	3
explain	why Americans were afraid of strong central government after years of British rule	1
describe	the strengths and weaknesses of the Articles of Confederation	2
summarize	how the Articles of Confederation gave each state freedom and independence from the central government, or Confederation of Congress	1
argue	the pros and cons of the Articles of Confederation	2
explain	when the Confederation of Congress became the United States of America	1
	two problems that made Americans realize their new government didn't have enough power	2
list arguments	for a strong national government and a strong state government	2
	for the Virginia Plan and the New Jersey Plan	2
make a Venn diagram	Virginia Plan, New Jersey Plan, Compromise of Both	3
describe	three accomplishments of the Constitutional Congress, May 1787	
compare and contrast	the Virginia Plan and the New Jersey Plan	2
	the concerns of large and small states	2
find	similarities and differences between the delegates to the Constitutional Convention	2
make a Venn diagram	of the Articles of Confederation, the Constitution, both	3
summarize	the Great Compromise and other compromises made at the Constitutional Convention	any number
explain	how the Constitution is permanent and yet changeable	2
	the system of checks and balances	2
describe	the importance of the Constitution, past and present	2
summarize	the seven articles of the Constitution	7
research	four or more of the 27 Amendments to the Constitution	4
sequence	the events that led to the development of the Constitution; its signing by the Constitutional delegates on September 17, 1787; its ratification; and its amendments	4
investigate	the who, what, when, where of one of the following: • Alexander Hamilton • James Madison • George Mason • Roger Sherman	4

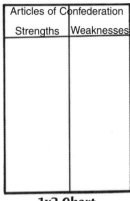

1x2 Chart

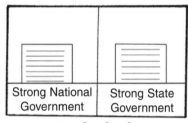

Pocket book

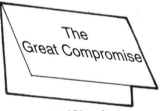

Three-tab Venn diagram

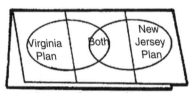

Half book

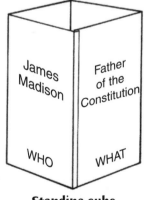

Standing cube

The New Nation

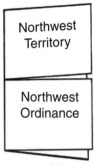

Northwest Territory

Northwest Ordinance

Two-tab book

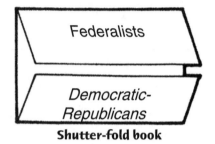

Federalists

Democratic-Republicans

Shutter-fold book

For Land Purchase	Against Land Purchase

1x2 Chart

U.S.A.: States in 1801

U.S.A.: States in 2001

Two-tab book

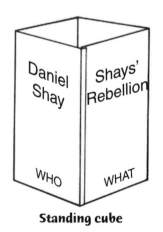

Daniel Shay

Shays' Rebellion

WHO

WHAT

Standing cube

Skill	Activity Suggestion	Foldable Parts
K-LK-L	ask yourself what you know, what you would like to know, and review what you learn about the first years of the new nation	3
make a table to show	attitudes towards the following before and after the revolution: • government--monarchy vs. republic • religion--separation of church and state • civil rights--Declaration of Rights • equality--slavery vs. abolition	3
describe	the Northwest Territory and the importance of the Northwest Ordinance of 1787	2
outline	the history of the District of Columbia and the city of Washington D.C.	2
research	the terms of the first five presidents of the new nation: • George Washington • John Adams • Thomas Jefferson • James Madison • James Monroe	5
chart	the views and beliefs of the nation's first political parties--Federalists and Democratic-Republicans	2
list	two reasons for rapid population growth after independence	2
argue	for and against the purchase of unknown land for $15 million dollars	2
map	the exploration route of the Lewis and Clark expedition, 1804-1806	1
compare and contrast	the center of the country in 1800 and today	2
list and describe	the sixteen states of the United States in 1801	16
research	the what, where, when, and why/how of the • Northwest Territory (1791) • President Washington's Proclamation of Neutrality (1793) • Whiskey Rebellion (1794) • Treaty of Greenville (1795) • Jay's Treaty (1794) • Pinckney's Treaty (1795) • Alien and Sedition Acts (1798) • Louisiana Purchase (1803)	4
investigate	the who, what, when, and where of one of the following: • Daniel Shay, Shays's Rebellion • Meriwether Lewis • William Clark	4

Economic Growth: Industrial Revolution

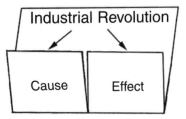

Two-tab concept map

Skill	Activity Suggestion	Foldable Parts
K-LK-L	ask yourself what you know, what you would like to know, and review what you learn about the Industrial Revolution	3
show	cause and effect of the Industrial Revolution	2
make a timeline	of the Industrial Revolution's beginning in Great Britain and growth in America: • 1750 British inventors designed machines to manufacture textiles • 1785 steam engine powered a cotton mill • 1789 Samuel Slater came to America with designs from Richard Arkwright's thread machines and began production • 1790 patent law passed by Congress • 1793 Eli Whitney invented the cotton gin • 1814 Francis Cabot Lowell developed a way to produce everything in one location, giving birth to the factory • add information	any number
make a Venn diagram	of the British Industrial Revolution, the American Industrial Revolution, both	3
list	ways in which the Industrial Revolution changed how people live and work	2
speculate	as to why the Industrial Revolution began in America about 1790, shortly after the American Revolution	any number
discuss	at least three reasons why the Industrial Revolution began in New England and flourished: • large population and work force • power to run machinery: water and coal • natural resources • good ports • capitalism and free-enterprise	3+
chart	positive and negative effects of the Industrial Revolution	2
	advantages and disadvantages of a free market	2
investigate	how the Industrial Revolution changed transportation on land and on water	2
	four inventions that strengthened the Industrial Revolution	4
explain	how faster production lowers costs of products	1
	the importance of interchangeable parts	1
show	the cause and effect of lower transportation costs and increased trade	2
investigate	the who, what, when, and where of one of the following: • Samuel Slater • Eli Whitney • Francis Cabot Lowell • Cyrus McCormick • John Deere • Robert Fulton	4
research	Massachusetts as the leading manufacturing state in the early 1800's, and determine the leading manufacturing state today	2
write	5 days of journal entries describing daily life as a worker in a factory	5

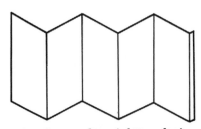

Timeline: Industrial Revolution

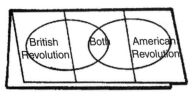

Three-tab Venn diagram

1x2 Chart

Four-tab book

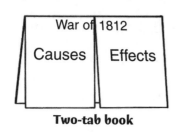

Two-tab book

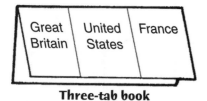

Three-tab book

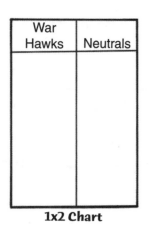

1x2 Chart

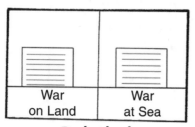

Pocket book

Half book

War of 1812

Skill	Activity Suggestion	Foldable Parts
K-LK-L	ask yourself what you know, what you would like to know, and review what you learn about the War of 1812	3
show	cause and effect of the War of 1812	2
make a timeline	of the major events of the War of 1812: • 1812, British navy blockaded America's east coast • 1812, July American General Hull retreated and surrendered Detroit to the British • 1812, August American frigate *Constitution* (Old Ironsides) destroyed the British vessel Guerriere • 1812, December American frigate *Constitution* destroyed the British vessel *Java* • 1813, September Oliver Hazard Perry defeated the British naval force on Lake Erie • 1813, October Battle of the Thames • 1813, Americans attacked York (Toronto) Canada • 1814, March Andrew Jackson defeated the Creeks at the Battle of Horseshoe Bend • 1814, August British forces took Washington, D.C. and burned the Capitol and president's mansion, but Americans recaptured the city • 1814, September British forces tried to take Baltimore, but were held off by bombardments from Fort McHenry (Francis Scott Key wrote the "Star Spangled Banner" during this battle) • 1814, September British defeat, Battle of Plattsburgh • 1814, December peace agreement, Treaty of Ghent • 1850, January Battle of New Orleans occurred after the end of the war, American victory led by Andrew Jackson	any number
describe	Great Britain, France, and United States involvement in the War of 1812	3
differentiate	between War Hawks and Neutrals	2
make a Venn diagram	of the British Navy, United States Navy, both	3
compare and contrast	the war on land and the war at sea	2
research	the role of Native Americans in this war	1
investigate	the what, where, when, and why of the following: • the Star Spangled Banner • USS Constitution also called "Old Ironsides"	4
	the who, what, when, where of one of the following: • Commodore Oliver Hazard Perry • Andrew Jackson • Francis Scott Key • Chief Tecumseh	4
describe	what it would have been like to be in Washington, D.C. as the British advanced and burned the city	1
explain	why the United States tried to invade Canada during the war	1
	the cause and effect of the Era of Good Feelings that followed the end of the War of 1812	2
summarize	three things the United States gained from this war	3

Expansion and the Monroe Doctrine

Skill	Activity Suggestion	Foldable Parts
K-LK-L	ask yourself what you know, what you would like to know, and review what you learn about westward expansion	3
show	cause and effect between the growing population of the United States and immigration to lands west of the Appalachian Mountains from 1770 to 1790	2
list	four reasons for westward expansion	4
investigate	the who, what, when, and where of one of the following: • Andrew Jackson • Daniel Boone • Abraham Lincoln	4
	the what, where, when, and how/why of one of the following: • the Wilderness Road • the Trail of Tears • the Treaty of Guadalupe Hidalgo (1848)	4
compare	attitudes towards Native Americans during the last half of the 1700's and the first half of the 1800's	2
identify	the land that was called Indian Territory and explain its purpose	2
research	the Cherokee, Choctaw, Chickasaw, Muscogee, and Seminole communities in the early 1800's	5
illustrate	how the western boundary of the United States changed over time: • Appalachian Mountains • Mississippi River • Rocky Mountains • Pacific Ocean	4
explain	how Texas and California became part of the U.S.A.	2
summarize	important events in Texas history that occurred on the following dates: 1821, 1836, 1845	3
describe	the importance of the discovery of gold in California in 1849	1
draw	maps that show the boundaries of the United States before and after the Mexican War	2
	maps that show the Oregon Trail, the Mormon Trail, and the California Trail and describe each	3
outline	the main events in the War with Mexico	any number
argue	for and against the idea of Manifest Destiny	2

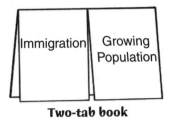

Two-tab book

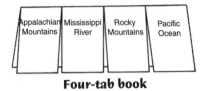

Four-tab book

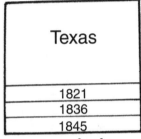

**Layer book
(2 sheets of paper)**

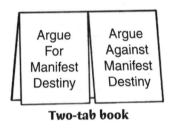

Two-tab book

Shutter-fold book

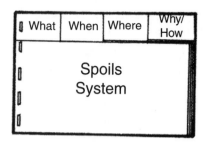

Top-tab book

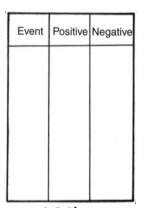

Bound book

Event	Positive	Negative

1x3 Chart

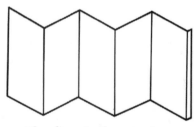

Timeline: Andrew Jackson

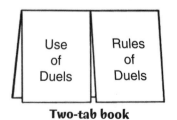

Two-tab book

The Jacksonian Era: 1824-1845

Skill	Activity Suggestion	Foldable Parts
K-LK-L	ask yourself what you know, what you would like to know, and review what you learn about the Andrew Jackson and the Jacksonian Era	3
read about and report on	Andrew Jackson's life before and after he became president of the United States	2
research	Andrew Jackson's involvement in the War of 1812 and the Battle of New Orleans	2
	and report on the positive and negative aspects of the presidential election of 1828	2
make a circle graph	Jackson received 56% of the popular vote	1
classify	events that occurred during Jackson's Presidency as either positive or negative for the nation	2
write	a biography of Andrew Jackson's life	1
explain	why Andrew Jackson was called "Old Hickory" and what the nickname says about his character	2
	how and why Jackson replaced the caucus system with nominating conventions	2
discuss	the positive expansion of suffrage during this time while noting which sections of the population were still not allowed to vote	2
define	*spoils system* and relate it to Jacksonians	2
make a timeline	of key events in Jackson's life and Presidency: • 1767, born in the Carolinas • 1796-1798, Tennessee Congressman • 1798, Tennessee state superior court judge • 1804, retired as a judge and worked with militia • 1804, 425 acre plantation called the Hermitage • 1806, fought a duel and killed Charles Dickenson • 1812, General in the War of 1812 • 1813-1814, The Creek War • 1815, Battle of New Orleans • 1817, Military Governor of Florida • 1824, political factions began to support Jackson • 1828, 7th President of the United States • 1829-1830, Indian Removal Act • 1832, 2nd term as president • 1832, Jackson wars against the Bank of the U.S. • 1836, Martin Van Buren, Jackson's VP and friend, is elected president • 1837, Panic of 1837, economic depression • 1838, Trail of Tears, result of Indian Removal Act • 1845, June died at his farm, the Hermitage	any number
research	the use of duels to solve disputes and describe the rules and etiquette that developed around dueling	2

Manifest Destiny

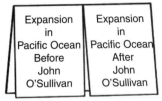

Two-tab book

Skill	Activity Suggestion	Foldable Parts
K-LK-L	ask yourself what you know, what you would like to know, and review what you learn about Manifest Destiny	3
describe	attitudes towards expansion to the Pacific Ocean before and after John O'Sullivan, a newspaper editor from New York, coined the term *Manifest Destiny*	2
investigate	the what, where, when, and why/how of the following: • Oregon Trail • California Trail • Santa Fe Trail • Mormon Trail • Old Spanish Trail • Conestoga wagon	4
make a timeline	of key events occurring between 1835 and 1850: • 1835, Texas began fight for independence • 1836, March Battle of the Alamo • 1836, April Battle of San Jacinto led to Texas independence from Mexico • 1839, Mexico's governor of California granted John Sutter 50,000 acres of land for a cattle ranch and trading post, Sutter's Fort • 1830's-1840's, mountain men and fur traders established trails into the western lands • 1841, Preemption Act passed to protect squatters • 1844, Brigham Young leads Mormons to Idaho • 1846, Texas became the 28th state • 1846, Oregon territory divided at 49th parallel • 1846, War with Mexico began • 1847, Mormons settled around the Great Salt Lake • 1848, Treaty of Hidalgo ended War with Mexico • 1850, 50,000+ emigrants on the Oregon Trail	any number
draw and label	a map that illustrates and explains the topography between the Mississippi River and the Pacific Ocean	2
explain	why the land west of the Mississippi was basically unknown and "overlanders" had to hire mountainmen or trailblazers as guides	2
write	a brochure that you could sell or give to other emigrants and explain the path you took to reach the west coast	3
	five journal entries relating a week in the life of a person traveling in a Conestoga wagon	5
report on	the Donner Party tragedy, 1846, and compare it to a recent survival event	2
research	and report on people who had ventured into this land and explain why they did so: • Kit Carson • Brigham Young • Marcus and Narcissa Whitman	any number
calculate	how long it would take to travel the full length of two of the westward trails if the wagons averaged 15 mph	2

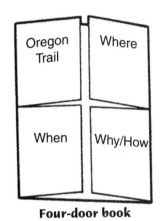

Four-door book

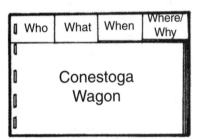

Top-tab book

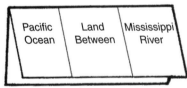

Three-tab book

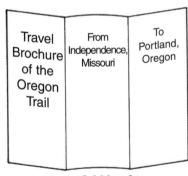

Trifold book

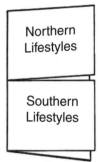

Northern Lifestyles

Southern Lifestyles

Two-tab book

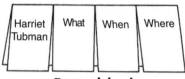

Harriet Tubman | What | When | Where

Four-tab book

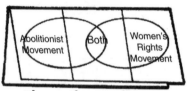

Abolitionist Movement | Both | Women's Rights Movement

Three-tab Venn diagram

Free States	Slave States

1x2 Chart

Daily Journal of a Freed Slave

Bound book

Slavery in America

Skill	Activity Suggestion	Foldable Parts
K-LK-L	ask yourself what you know, what you would like to know, and review what you learn about slavery in America	3
compare	lifestyles in the northern and southern regions of the United States in the mid-1800's	2
	the needs of a manufacturing society to the needs of an agricultural society	2
describe	opportunities for work in the North and the South	2
explain	how the question of slavery deeply divided the United States in the 1850's	1
list	some of the arguments for and against slavery	2
make a Venn diagram	of lives of free African Americans, lives of enslaved African Americans, and both	3
compare and contrast	attitudes towards African Americans in the North and in the South before the Civil War	2
search the web	for information on past and present African American publications	2
define and describe	the abolitionist movement	2
investigate	the who, what, when, where of one of the following: • Nat Turner • Frederick Douglass • William Lloyd Garrison • Angelina Grimke and Sarah Grimke • Harriet Tubman • Levi Coffin and Catherine Coffin • Sojourner Truth • Harriet Beecher Stowe • John Brown	4
	the what, when, where, why/how of one of the following: • *Freedom's Journal* • Underground Railroad • *The Liberator*, an abolitionist newspaper • Harper's Ferry • Dred Scott decision of 1857 • *Uncle Tom's Cabin*	4
make a Venn diagram	of the Abolitionist Movement, the Women's Rights Movement, both	3
chart	free states and slave states in the 1850's	2
summarize	the Missouri Compromise of 1820, the Compromise of 1850, and the Kansas-Nebraska Act of 1854	3
research	attitudes towards the Dred Scott decision in 1857 and 1866	2
outline	the Thirteenth, Fourteenth, and Fifteenth Amendments to the Constitution and explain their importance	3
write	5 days of journal entries made by a slave who has just been informed of their freedom	5
	a biography of the life of a freed slave	1

The Civil War

Skill	Activity Suggestion	Foldable Parts
K-LK-L	ask yourself what you know, what you would like to know, and review what you learn about the Civil War	3
list	and describe the first seven states that seceded to form the Confederate States of America	7
show	cause and effect of Abraham Lincoln's being elected President in 1860	2
	differing opinions on states' rights and slavery	2
describe	events occurring before, during, and after the Civil War	3
	the armies of the North and the South	2
	two ways in which blockades are used in war	2
	three ways in which advancements in technology changed the way this war was fought	3
list	Northern and Southern victories	2
make a timeline	of the key events of the Civil War	any number
compare	the strengths and weaknesses of the North and South	4
graph	the percentage of Southerners who owned slaves	1
describe in detail	two of the battles of the Civil War: Antietam, Shiloh, Vicksburg, Gettysburg, others	2
research	the who, what, when, where of one of the following: • Abraham Lincoln • Jefferson Davis • Robert E. Lee • Ulysses S. Grant • Rose Greenhow, Confederate spy • Blance Bruce and Hiram Revels • William Tecumseh Sherman • Robert Gould Shaw	4
	the what, where, when, why/how of one of the following: • Fort Summer • *Monitor* and the *Merrimack* • Emancipation Proclamation • Gettysburg Address • Appomattox, Virginia • Freedman's Bureau	4
make a Venn diagram	to compare the American Revolution, the Civil War, both	3
	Ulysses Grant, Robert E. Lee, both	3
summarize	the Thirteenth, Fourteenth, and Fifteenth Amendments	3
write	about the meaning of "With malice toward none, with charity for all."	1
research and report on	the 54th Massachusetts Colored Regiment	1

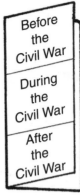

Three-tab book

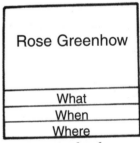

3x3 Table

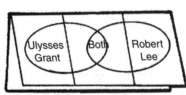

Layer book (2 sheets of paper)

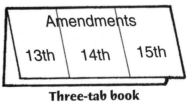

Three-tab Venn diagram

United States History 65

Reconstruction

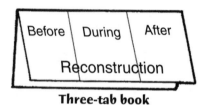

Standing cube

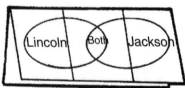

Three-tab book

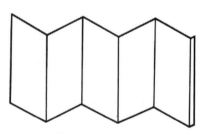

Three-tab Venn diagram

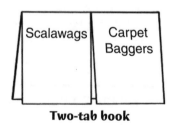

Timeline: Reconstruction

Scalawags | Carpet Baggers

Two-tab book

Skill	Activity Suggestion	Foldable Parts
K-LK-L	ask yourself what you know, what you would like to know, and review what you learn about reconstruction after the Civil War	3
list	four reasons for serious economic problems after the war ended: • severe property damage • crops not planted, fields in ruin • transportation routes had been destroyed • many adult males killed or disabled during the war • reduction in workforce • freed slaves needed economic help	4
describe	how Reconstruction affected blacks and whites in the South	2
outline	events before, during, and after Reconstruction	3
research and report on	the pros and cons of each of the following three plans for reconstruction: • Ten Percent Plan, December 1863 • Wade-Davis Bill, July 1864 • Restoration, Summer 1865	2 2 2
make a Venn diagram	President Lincoln's views on reconstruction with President Andrew Johnson's views, both	3
make a timeline	of key events in Reconstruction: • 1863, December Ten Percent Plan for Reconstruction proposed by President Lincoln • 1864, July Wade-Davis Plan for Reconstruction • 1865, January Thirteenth Amendment abolishing slavery passed • 1865, March Lincoln formed *Freedman's Bureau* • 1865, April 9 Lee surrendered to Grant • 1865, April 14 President Lincoln assassinated, Vice President Andrew Johnson became president • 1865, Restoration program for Reconstruction • 1865, Fall former Confederate states formed new governments and elected new representatives • 1865, prejudicial laws called *black codes* passed • 1866, Freedman's Bureau's powers extended • 1866, Civil Rights Act of 1866 gave African Americans full citizenship and nullified the 1857 Dred Scott decision • 1866, Fourteenth Amendment passed Congress • 1867, March Radical Reconstruction started First Reconstruction Act passed Second Reconstruction Act passed • 1868, Fourteenth Amendment finally adopted • 1868, most Southern states readmitted to Union • 1868, Ulysses S. Grant elected president • 1870, February Fifteenth Amendment became law • 1872, May the Amnesty Act passed	any number
explain	how President Johnson's views on reconstruction and his response to the Tenure of Office Act led to his impeachment trial	2
	the roles scalawags and carpetbaggers played in Reconstruction	2
compare	past and present terrorists groups	2

Go West: The Frontier

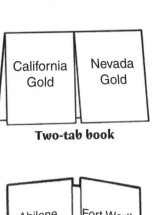

Two-tab book

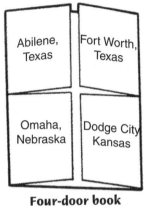

Four-door book

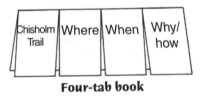

Four-tab book

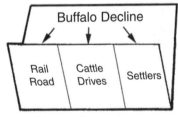

Three-tab concept map

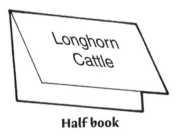

Half book

Skill	Activity Suggestion	Foldable Parts
K-LK-L	ask yourself what you know, what you would like to know, and review what you learn about the American frontier	3
make a timeline	of the key events in the building of the first transcontinental railroad	any number
	to show key events in the Plains War	any number
	of the short life of the pony express	any number
	of the history of the 20 year "Cattle Kingdom" period beginning in the late 1860's and lasting until the 1880's	any number
	of the history of longhorn cattle	any number
locate on a map or globe	gold discoveries in Colorado and Nevada, 1858	2
	three areas where homesteaders established new towns during the 1860's	3
	three cattle towns: • Abilene, Texas; Fort Worth, Texas; Dodge City, Kansas; Omaha, Nebraska, others	3
describe	how construction of the transcontinental railroad started on the East and West coasts and met at a point in the middle of the country	2
list	four problems encountered while building the transcontinental railroad and their solutions	4
show cause and effect	of the transcontinental railroad and the economic growth of the West and the entire United States	2
explain	how railroads made travel faster, cheaper, and safer	3
research	the what, where, when, why/how of one of the following: • Promontory Point, Utah • Chisholm Trail • Homestead Act of 1862 • Goodnight-Loving Trail	4
	the who, what, when, where of one of the following: • Grenville Dodge • Charles Crocker • Chief Joseph • George Custer	4
make a Venn diagram	to compare Native Americans, settlers, both	3
make a concept map	showing the decline of buffalo due to railroads, cattle drives, and new settlers	3
describe	two ways in which the cattle industry changed the western frontier	2

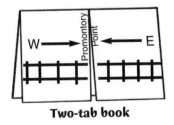

Two-tab book

Urbanization

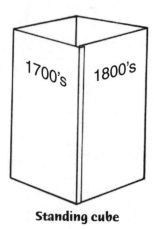

Standing cube

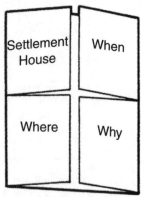

Four-door book

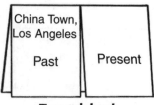

Two-tab book

Skill	Activity Suggestion	Foldable Parts
K-LK-L	ask yourself what you know, what you would like to know, and review what you learn about the urbanization of America	3
graph	the percentage of Americans living on a farm in 1800, 1900, 2000	3
explain	the following shifts in American lifestyles: • rural to urban (to find work) • rural to suburb (to get away from overcrowded cities) • suburb to rural (to get back to basics) • suburb to urban (to rejuvenate the city)	3
compare and contrast	any of the following: • life in rural and urban areas in the 1700's • life in rural and urban areas in the 1800's • life in rural and urban areas in the 1900's • life in rural and urban areas at present	2
investigate	the what, where, when, why/how of the following: • settlement houses • the "Gilded Age" of the late 1800's	
list	reasons cities grow and cities decline	2
speculate	as to why immigrants tend to move to cities, and why they tend to settle together as ethnic groups	2
	as to why many Americans resented immigrants in the work force, and why they discriminated against them	2
search the web	for information on the past and present status of famous ethnic areas within large cities: • Chinatown, Los Angeles, California • Little Italy, New York City, New York • others	2
investigate	America's current population distribution	4
predict	future trends in population distribution in two American cities	2

Compare	Current Population Trend	Predicting Population Trend
City #1		
City #2		

3x3 Table

Immigration

Skill	Activity Suggestion	Foldable Parts
K-LK-L	ask yourself what you know, what you would like to know, and review what you learn about immigration to America	3
define	immigrant and emigrant	1
make a timeline	to show key events in the history of American immigration: • Naturalization Act of 1790, stipulated that "any alien, being a free white person, may be admitted to become a citizen of the United States" • 1891 The Federal Government assumed the task of inspecting, admitting, rejecting, and processing all immigrants seeking admission to the U.S. • 1917 Act Required that immigrants be able to read and write in their native language. • 1921, National Origins Act, established a quota system and reduced the annual country quota from 3% to 2% and based it upon the low 1890 census • 1940 The Alien Registration Act required all aliens (non-U.S. citizens) within the United States to register with the Government and receive an Alien Registration Receipt Card (the predecessor of the "green card"). • 1968 Act Eliminated immigration discrimination based on race, place of birth, sex and residence. It also officially abolished restrictions on Asian immigration. • 1986 Act Focused on curtailing illegal immigration. It legalized hundred of thousands of illegal immigrants. It also introduced the employer sanctions program which fines employers for hiring illegal workers. It also passed tough laws to prevent bogus marriage fraud.	any number
describe	the impact of immigration and immigrants on a city	2
	settlement houses, slums, and tenements	3
	three reasons people immigrate from one place to another	3
	what was meant by the terms "old country" and "new country"	2
research	Ellis Island and Angel Island and explain their importance	2
	the who, what, when, where of one of the following: • Jane Addams • Pauline Newman • Grace Abott and Julia Clifford Lathrop	4
	the what, when, where, why/how of one of the following: • the Great Chicago Fire • Hull House, the first settlement house	4
outline	two or more things immigrants had to do before they were allowed to enter the country	2
document	past and present efforts to limit immigration to America	2
interview	someone who has recently immigrated to the United States and report on their experiences	2

Two-tab book

Three-tab book

Shutter-fold book

Two-tab concept map

Half book

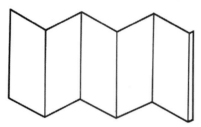

Timeline: Inventions and Technology

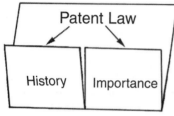

Two-tab concept map

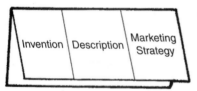

Three-tab book

1. How did the electric light-bulb change the lifestyles of early Americans?

Three-quarter book

Compare	Life Before	Life After
Invention #1		
Invention #2		

3x3 Table

Inventions and Technology

Skill	Activity Suggestion	Foldable Parts
K-LK-L	ask yourself what you know, what you would like to know, and review what you learn about changes brought on by inventions and technology	3
make a timeline	outlining key events in the history of inventions	4
present	five examples of how inventions have changed the world since prehistoric times	5
explain	how inventions can change lifestyles for better and for worse	2
	how inventions can change the economy of a country	1
research	the history of patent law and explain its importance	2
investigate	the who, what, when, where of one of the following: • Benjamin Franklin • Thomas Alva Edison • Alexander Graham Bell • Lewis Latimer • Elijah McCoy • Orville Wright and Wilbur Wright • Henry Ford	4
	the what, when, where, why/how of the following: • inventions of the 1700's • inventions of the 1800's • inventions of the 1900's	4
invent	something, describe your invention, and plan marketing and promotion strategies	3
predict	how future inventions might change civilization	1
outline	how inventions and technology changed the following: • transportation • communication • manufacturing • agriculture • cooking and house cleaning • military operations • medical care, others	any number
show cause and effect	of an invention taken for granted today: • pencil • bicycle • plastic • steel • Teflon • adhesive • latex paint, others	2
describe	life before and after an important invention, such as electricity	2

Business and Industry

Skill	Activity Suggestion	Foldable Parts
K-LK-L	ask yourself what you know, what you would like to know, and review what you learn about the growth of business and industry in America	3
investigate	when the economy of the United States was based upon agriculture and explain why	2
	when the economy of the United States shifted to an industrial economy and explain why	2
make a timeline	to show the growth of business and industry at the end of the 19th century and the beginning of the 20th century	any number
outline	the history of the use of iron and steel	any number
	the history of the labor movement and unions	any number
	the reform movement to eliminate and control unfair business practices	any number
explain	the cause and effect of prosperity during the 1920's	2
	how technological advances led to the growth of large companies	1
describe	important reforms in the food industry, manufacturing, and mining	3
list	pros and cons of a monopoly	2
	reasons monopolies are built and broken	2
make a Venn diagram	to compare a corporation, partnership, both	3
	to compare factory workers, farm workers, both	3
compare and contrast	growth of the steel industry, the oil industry, manufacturing	3
	past and present use of child labor in America and the world	2
	jobs available for workers in the 1700's, 1800's, 1900's 2000's	3
investigate	the who, what, when, where of any of the following: • Andrew Carnegie • John D. Rockefeller • J. P. Morgan • Mary Harris Jones • Samuel Conpers	4
	the what, when, where, why/how of any of the following: • American Federation of Labor, AFL • Sherman Anti-Trust Act, 1890 • assembly lines • labor unions and collective bargaining	4
make a Venn diagram	the growth of industry in the United States, the growth of industry in another country, both	3
research	the past and present environmental impact of industry	2
	the industrial revolution that occurred in the 1920's	1

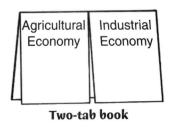

Two-tab book

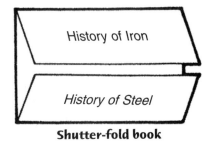

Shutter-fold book

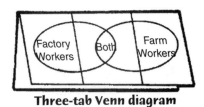

Three-tab Venn diagram

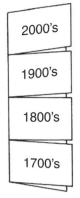

Four-tab book

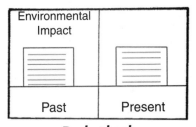

Pocket book

Reform...

| Big Business |
| Government |
| Equal Rights |
| Working Conditions |
| Urban |

Layer book
(3 sheets of paper)

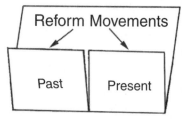

Reform Movements

Past   Present

Two-tab concept map

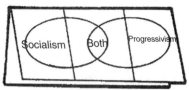

Socialism   Both   Progressivism

Three-tab Venn diagram

What:
Square
Deal   When:
            1904

Standing cube

urbanization
muckraker
patronage
trusts
suffragists
reform
prohibition
laissez-faire
conservation
arbitration

Vocabulary
book

The Progressive Movement

Skill	Activity Suggestion	Foldable Parts
K-LK-L	ask yourself what you know, what you would like to know, and review what you learn about the Progressive movement for reform	3
define	and give past and present examples of the following: • reform movements • muckrakers • kickbacks • political machines and political bosses	2
describe	why a movement that called for reforms was needed in each of the following: • big business reform • government reform • equal rights reform • working conditions reform • urban reform	5
research	the importance of journalists exposing corruption and unfair practices--past and present	2
make a timeline	of key events in the Progressive Movement: • 1877-1881, President Rutherfold B. Hayes tried to reform the civil service without support • 1881, President James Garfield hoped to reform civil service, but was assassinated • 1883, Civil Service Commission established to control the hiring of federal employees • 1887, Interstate Commerce Art passed Interstate Commerce Commission created • 1890, Sherman Antitrust Act passed • 1890, National American Woman Suffrage Association started • 1893, President Grover Cleveland, lower tariffs • 1906, Meat Inspection Act passed • 1906, Pure Food and Drug Act passed • 1913, Sixteenth Amendment, income tax • 1913, Seventeenth Amendment ratified giving citizens the right to vote for their representatives • 1913, Federal Reserve Act passed • 1913, tariff reform finally achieved • 1914, Federal Trade Commission established • 1914, Clayton Antitrust Act • 1919, Eighteenth Amendment ratified • 1920, Nineteenth Amendment ratified	any number
determine	who did and did not benefit from the spoils system	2
investigate	the who, what, when, where of the following: • Lincoln Steffens, *The Shame of the City (1904)* • Ida Tarbell, *The History of the Standard Oil Company* • Upton Sinclair, *The Jungle (1906)* • Anna Howard Shaw and Carrie Chapman Catt	4
	the what, where, when, why/how of the following: • the Oregon System • Square Deal	4
make a Venn diagram	• President Theodore Roosevelt, President William Howard Taft, both Progressive Presidents • socialism, progressivism, both	3
give	10 examples of how reforms initiated during this time directly influence your life today	10

Overseas Expansion

Skill	Activity Suggestion	Foldable Parts
K-LK-L	ask yourself what you know, what you would like to know, and review what you learn about the expansion of the United States	3
make a timeline	of the history of either Alaska or Hawaii	any number
	of the history of the Panama Canal	any number
describe	new territories gained by the United States in the late 1800's	
compare and contrast	Alaska and Hawaii before and after they became states	2
identify	two causes of the Spanish-American War (1898)	2
analyze	two consequences of the Spanish-American War	2
investigate	three territories the United States gained in the Spanish-American War: • Puerto Rico, Guam, and the Philippines	3
locate on a map	the lands controlled by the United States by 1900: • Alaska, Aleutian Islands, Hawaiian Islands, • Johnston Island, Baker Island, American Samoa, • Wake Island, Midway Islands, Guam, Phillippine Islands, Puerto Rico	11
investigate	the who, what, when, where of one of the following: • James Cook • Queen Liliuokalani • William Seward • William McKinley • Theodore Roosevelt • George Dewey	4
chart	the pros and cons of the United States buying a 10-mile-wide strip of land called the Panama Canal Zone	2
research	why the United States bought the Virgin Islands from Denmark during World War I	1

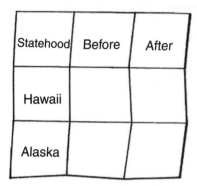

3x3 Table

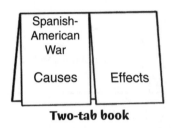

Two-tab book

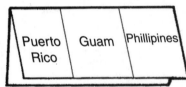

Three-tab book

Shutter-fold book

World War I

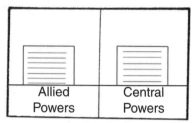

Pocket book

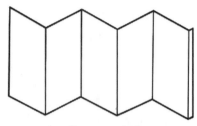

Timeline: World War I

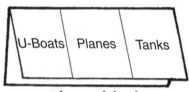

Three-tab book

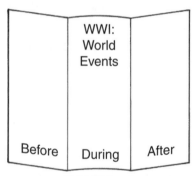

Trifold book

League of Nations	
For	Against

1x2 Chart

Skill	Activity Suggestion	Foldable Parts
K-LK-L	ask yourself what you know, what you would like to know, and review what you learn about World War I	3
compare	the Allied Powers and the Central Powers	2
make a timeline	of some of the key events of World War I • 1914, June 28 Franz Ferdinand was assassinated • 1914, June World War I began • 1914, September 5 Battle of the Marne • 1914, April poison gas first used by the Germans • 1915, May 7 Lusitania torpedoed by Germany • 1916, February Battle of Verdun • 1916, May Battle of Somme • 1916, January armored tanks first used in war • 1917, April 6 United States entered the war • 1918, July Battle of the Argonne Forest • 1918, November 11 World War I ends • 1919, June 28 Treaty of Versailles signed • 1920, U.S. Senate rejected League of Nations	any number
locate	the following on a map or globe: • Britain, France, Italy, Belgium and Russia (Allies)	5
	• Germany, Austria-Hungary, Turkey (Central Powers)	3
explain	two key events that led the United States into WWI	2
outline	three things Woodrow Wilson said the United States should fight for	3
describe	two ways in which World War I changed the United States	2
	world events before, during, and after WWI	3
research	the design and use of German U-boats, war planes, and tanks	3
debate	the use of poison gas as a weapon	1
argue	for and against the United States joining the League of Nations after World War I	2
list	examples of difficulties faced on the war front and the home front	2
investigate	the who, what, when, where of one of the following: • Archduke Franz Ferdinand • Woodrow Wilson • Eddie Rickenbacker, American pilot • Baron von Richthofen, "Red Baron," German pilot	4
	the what, where, when, why/how, of one of the following: • Lusitania • Zimmermann telegram • the Treaty of Versailles • the League of Nations • Veteran's Day	4
research	and report on one of the military firsts of WWI: • use of poison gas • armored tanks • airplanes • zeppelins, or blimps • others	1
Venn diagram	submarines, German U-boats, both	3

Between World Wars: 1920's

Skill	Activity Suggestion	Foldable Parts
K-LK-L	ask yourself what you know, what you would like to know, and review what you learn about the years between World War I and World War II	3
make a timeline	of some of the key events during this time: • late 1919-1920, Red Scare • 1920's, stock market boom • 1920, Eighteenth Amendment, Prohibition • 1920, Nineteenth Amendment, gave women the right to vote • 1924, National Origins Act passed • 1925, Scopes Trial • 1927, first "talkie" movie (a movie with sound) • 1927, Lindbergh flew solo across the Atlantic • 1927, Babe Ruth hit 60 home runs • 1928, Kellogg-Briad Pact signed by 15 nations	any number
outline	the rise and fall of Prohibition	2
research	the rapid growth of three types of media during this time: radio, newspapers, magazines	3
show	cause and effect between growth in the media and growth in the advertising industry	2
	cause and effect between improved transportation and an increase in travel	2
describe	key events in each of the three terms of President Franklin D. Roosevelt	3
research	the first non-stop, solo flight across the Atlantic, completed by Charles Lindbergh in May 1917	1
compare and contrast	methods of communication in the 1920's and today	2
	methods of transportation in the 1920's and today	2
	celebrities of the 1920's and today	2
explain	two ways in which women's lives changed during this time	2
investigate	the who, what, when, where of any of the following: • Calvin Coolidge and/or Franklin D. Roosevelt • J. Edgar Hoover • Charles Lindbergh and/or Amelia Earhart • Duke Ellington, Louis Armstrong, or Bessie Smith • A. Philip Randolph and/or Marcus Garvey • F. Scott Fitzgerald, and/or Gertrude Stein • Babe Ruth • Al Capone	4
	the what, when, where, why/how of one of the following: • the Jazz Age, 1920's • the Red Scare, 1919-1920 • "flappers", 1920's • Teapot Dome Scandal, 1922 • Brotherhood of Sleeping Car Porters, 1920's • Kellogg-Braid Pact, 1928	4

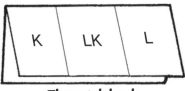

Three-tab book

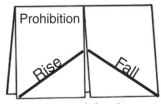

Two-tab book

Three-tab book

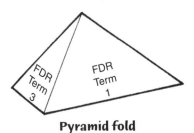

Pyramid fold

3x3 Table

The Great Depression and the 1930's

Four-door book

| Hoover Dam | When |
| Where | Why |

Four-door book

Explain	Past Effects	Present Effects
Great Depression		
New Deal		

3x3 Table

| Another Great Depression | |
| Possible | Impossible |

1x2 Chart

Stock Market Journal

Bound book

Skill	Activity Suggestion	Foldable Parts
K-LK-L	ask yourself what you know, what you would like to know, and review what you learn about the Great Depression	3
make a timeline	of key events of the Great Depression: • 1929, Stock Market Crash • 1930, October 24, Great Depression began called "Black Thursday" • 1930, Drought over Great Plains • 1932, 25% unemployment • 1932, Franklin Roosevelt elected president • 1933, Emergency Banking Relief Act • 1933, Hundred Days, Congress approved 15 new programs during a special session Roosevelt's New Deal began • 1933, Hilter rose to power in Germany • 1934, Indian Reorganization Act passed • 1935, Social Security Act passed • 1935, Second New Deal • 1936, FDR reelected, economy not recovered • 1939, World War II begins	any number
describe	two causes of the Great Depression	2
outline	three ways in which the Federal government changed during the New Deal	3
	three actions taken under the New Deal	3
imagine	life before, during, and after the Dust Bowl	3
	life before, during, and after the Great Depression	3
explain	how both grazing and farming made the effects of the drought worse by destroying the grass cover	2
	past and present effects of the New Deal	2
investigate	the who, what, when, where of one of the following: • Herbert Hoover • Franklin D. Roosevelt • Eleanor Roosevelt • Frances Perkins • Hattie Caraway	4
	the what, where, when, why/how of one of the following: • Dust Bowl • Black Tuesday • The New Deal • Hoover Dam	4
discuss	whether it would or would not be possible for America to experience another "Great Depression"	2
follow	the movement of the stockmarket over a period of 5 or more days and analyze your findings	5+
explain	any of the following New Deal programs: • Civilian Conservation Corps (CCC) • Federal Emergency Relief Administration (FERA) • Agricultural Adjustment Act (AAA) • Tennessee Valley Authority (TVA) • National Recovery Administration (NRA) • Public Works Administration (PWA) • Federal Deposit Insurance Corporation (FDIC) • Securities and Exchange Commission (SEC) • Social Security Act of 1935	any number

World War II

Skill	Activity Suggestion	Foldable Parts
K-LK-L	ask yourself what you know, what you would like to know, and review what you learn about World War II	3
make a timeline	of some key events of World War II: • 1939, September World War II began; Hitler invaded Poland • 1940, August Germany bombs Britain • 1941, June Hitler attacks the Soviet Union • 1941, December 7 Japan bombed Pearl Harbor • 1941, December U.S. declared war on Japan • 1941, December Germany and Italy, allies of Japan, declared war on U.S. • 1942, January United States joined Allies • 1942, April Allies surrendered Bataan • 1944, June 6 Battle of Normandy, D-Day Invasion • 1944, December Battle of the Bulge • 1945, March Battle of Iwo Jima • 1945, May Germany surrendered • 1945, June Battle of Okinawa • 1945, August Atomic bomb dropped on Hiroshima • 1945, August 15 V-J Day, "Victory over Japan" • 1945, September 3 Japan's formally surrendered • World War II ended	any number
sequence	three events that occurred on December 7, 1941	3
compare and contrast	World War II before and after United States involvement	2
	democracy and communism	2
list	pros and cons of United States involvement	2
locate	the following on a map or globe: • Pearl Harbor, Island of Oahu, Hawaii • Hiroshima, Japan • Nagasaki, Japan	3
differentiate	between the Axis countries and the Allied countries	2
make a concept map	on dictators--Hitler, Stalin, and Mussolini	3
	on World War II Fronts--Pacific/Asian and European	2
	of World War II Countries--Axis, Allied, Neutral	3
describe	the American economy before, during, and after World War II	3
	the goals of the United Nations--past and present	2
outline	arguments for and against the use of relocation camps	2
research	four battles of World War II	4
list	three effects of World War II on the world	3
research	the who, what, when, where of one of the following: • Franklin D. Roosevelt • Adolf Hitler • Josef Stalin • Benito Mussolini • Winston Churchill • Dwight D. Eisenhower • Harry S. Truman	4
	the what, where, when, why/how of one of the following: • Pearl Harbor • atomic bomb • Holocaust • concentration camps • American relocation camps	4

Shutter-fold book

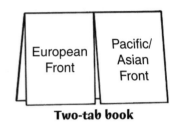

Two-tab book

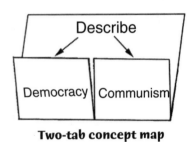

Two-tab concept map

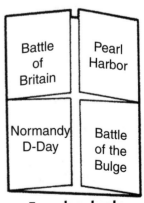

Three-tab concept map

Four-door book

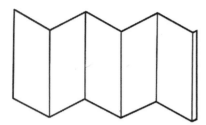

Timeline: Cold War

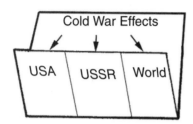

Three-tab concept map

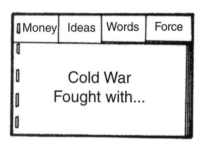

Top-tab book

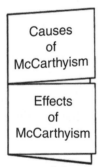

Two-tab book

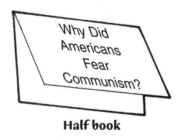

Half book

The Cold War

Skill	Activity Suggestion	Foldable Parts
K-LK-L	ask yourself what you know, what you would like to know, and review what you learn about the Cold War	3
make a timeline	of key events of the 40-year Cold War • 1946, Cold War, a rivalry between super powers, began after WWII • 1953, Soviet dictator, Joseph Stalin died Nikita Khrushchev took his place • 1954, the Arms Race escalated • 1955, July Geneva summit, policy of "peaceful coexistence" began • 1957, Russia launched the satellite *Sputnik* • 1958, U.S. failed in launch of satellite *Vanguard*, • 1958, U.S.A. launched satellite *Explorer* • 1959, Khrushchev visited the United States • 1960, May 1 U-2 plane was shot down by Soviets pilot captured, tensions rise • 1960, May 16 summit in Paris lasted one day Cold War "thaw" was over • 1961, Bay of Pigs • 1962, Cuban Missile Crisis, serious cold war dispute • 1963, "hotline" linked Washington to Moscow • 1972, Strategic Arms Limitation Treaty, SALT 1 • 1979, Strategic Arms Limitation Treaty, SALT II, not approved when Soviet troops invaded Afghanistan • 1985, Mikhail Gorbachev, new Soviet leader • 1987, Intermediate-Range Nuclear Forces Treaty, INF • 1991, Strategic Arms Reduction Treaty, START • 1991, December 25 end of Soviet Union	any number
locate	the former Soviet Union on a map or globe	1
explain	how the Cold War was fought with ideas, money, words, and force	4
	what part the space program played in the Cold War	1
make a concept map	superpowers--United States and Soviet Union	2
find	similarities and differences between the United States and the Soviet Union	2
list	Europe's communist and noncommunist countries and draw the Iron Curtain between the countries on your list	2
describe	the effects of the Cold War on the United States and the World	2
	Richard Nixon's historic visits to China (1972) and the Soviet Union (1972) and explain how they eased Cold War tensions	2
	how and why the Cold War ended	2
show	cause and effect of the arms race	2
	cause and effect of McCarthyism	2
summarize	why many Americans feared communism	1
investigate	the who, what, when, where of one of the following: • Harry S. Truman • Dwight D. Eisenhower • Joseph McCarthy	4
	the what, where, when, why/how of one of the following: • Iron Curtain • NATO, North Atlantic Treaty Organization • Sputnik	4

The Korean War

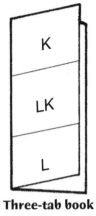

Three-tab book

Skill	Activity Suggestion	Foldable Parts
K-LK-L	ask yourself what you know, what you would like to know, and review what you learn about the Korean War	3
make a timeline	of key events of the Korean War: • 1950, June 25 North Korea invaded South Korea • 1950, June 27 U.S. air and naval forces ordered to help defend South Korea • 1950, June 30 ground troops arrived • 1950, September 8 Allied troops stopped communist advance at Pusan Perimeter • 1950, September 15 Allied troops landed at Inchon • 1950, September 26 Allies captured Seoul • 1950, October 19 Allies captured North Korean capital • 1950, October 25 China supported North Korea • 1950, November 26 Allies battled Chinese • 1951, January 4 Communists occupied Seoul • 1951, March 14 Allies reoccupied Seoul • 1951, April 11 General MacArthur replaced by General Ridgway • 1951, July 10 truce talks began • 1952, April 28 communist negotiators rejected proposal for voluntary repatriation of prisoners • 1952, October 8 truce talks stopped • 1953, March 29 communists accepted U.N. proposal to exchange sick and wounded prisoners • 1953, April 26 truce talks resumed • 1953, July 27 Armistice agreement signed, Korean War ended	any number
locate	the following on a map or globe: • North Korea • South Korea • Seoul, South Korea's capital city • Pyongyang, North Korea's capital city • China	5
compare and contrast	North Korean and South Korean governments--past and present	2
investigate	the who, what, when, where of one of the following: • General Douglas MacArthur • President Truman	4
	the what, when, where, why/how of one of the following: • 38th parallel of latitude • United Nations • demilitarized zone	4
explain	why the Korean War is said to be one of the bloodiest wars of all time	1

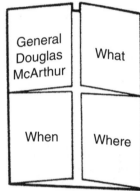

Four-door book

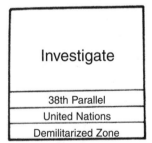

3x3 Table

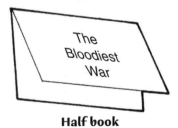

Layer book
(2 sheets of paper)

Half book

Civil and Equal Rights

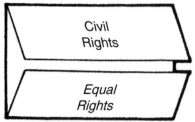

Shutter-fold book

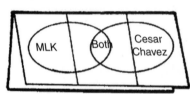

1x2 Chart

Three-tab Venn diagram

Progressive Movement Helped Women

NAWSA

Womens Trade Union

Childrens Bureau

Layer book (2 sheets of paper)

Personal Interviews Regarding Civil Rights Issues

Bound book

Skill	Activity Suggestion	Foldable Parts
K-LK-L	ask yourself what you know, what you would like to know, and review what you learn about civil and equal rights	3
make a timeline	of key events in the Civil Rights Movement	any number
	of key events in the Equal Rights Movement	any number
define	and give examples of discrimination	2
	and give two examples of segregation	2
	suffrage and suffragists	2
locate and explain	the path of the Great Migration	1
show	cause and effect of the increase in African American migration to large cities in the northern United States during World War I	2
list	pros and cons of demonstrations and marches	2
compare	civil rights and equal rights	2
make a Venn diagram	of the Civil Rights Movement, the Equal Rights Movement, both	3
	of Martin Luther King, Jr., Cesar Chavez, both	3
	of the Civil Rights Act, 1964; Voting Rights Act, 1965; both	3
discuss	gains made in equal rights for senior citizens, women, and people with disabilities	3
summarize	Brown versus Board of Education	1
investigate	the Gray Panthers and Maggie Kuhn	2
outline	the conception, conditions, and implementation of the Americans with Disabilities Act, or ADA	3
discuss	two ways in which the Progressive movement helped women: • National American Woman Suffrage Association formed (1890) and 19th Amendment passed (1919) • Women's Trade Union League (1903) formed • Children's Bureau formed in the Labor Department (1912), others	2
research	the who, what, when, where of one of the following: • Booker T. Washington • Susan B. Anthony • Dr. Martin Luther King, Jr. • Rosa Parks • Thurgood Marshall • Malcolm X • Cesar Chavez and Dolores Huerta	4
	the what, where, when, why/how of one of the following: • The Great Migration • National Association for the Advancement of Colored People, NAACP • Eighteenth Amendment, 1919 • Nineteenth Amendment, 1920 • League of Women Voters • Watts Riots, 1965 • La Causa, "The Cause"	4
interview	four people in your community to determine attitudes towards current civil rights issues and record findings	4

Vietnam Era

Skill	Activity Suggestion	Foldable Parts
K-LK-L	ask yourself what you know, what you would like to know, and review what you learn about the events occurring between 1960 and 1975	3
research	and report on any 4 key events of the 1960's: • Sputnik, 1957 • National Aeronautics and Space Administration • Bay of Pigs, 1961 • Peace Corp created, 1961 • Cuban missile crisis, 1962 • Alan Shepard, Jr. and/or John Glenn, early 1960's • Neil Armstrong become first person to walk on the moon, 1969	4
make a timeline	of key events of the Vietnam War: • 1957, Viet Cong rebeled against South Vietnamese government and Ngo Dinh Diem • 1959, Civil War in Vietnam • 1963, South Vietnamese generals overthrew the Diem government • 1964, Congress passed the Tonkin Gulf Resolution • 1965, President Johnson sent first ground troops • 1968, North Vietnam and Viet Cong launched a campaign against South Vietnamese cities--Tet Offensive • 1969, President Nixon announced that U.S. troops would begin to withdraw from Vietnam • 1970, Kent State shootings occurred • 1973, cease-fire agreement signed • 1973, U.S. ground troops left Vietnam, Paris Peace Accords • 1975, South Vietnam surrendered, the war ends	any number
locate	the following countries on a map or globe: • North Vietnam • South Vietnam • Cambodia	3
analyze	the causes and effects of the Vietnam War	2
compare and contrast	North Vietnam and South Vietnam before and after the war	2
make a Venn diagram	comparing war "Hawks," "Doves," and both	3
research	the who, what, when, where of one of the following: • Ho Chi Minh • Fidel Castro	4
	the what, where, when, why/how of one of the following: • Berlin Wall • Green Berets • anti-war protests • Tet offensive • Kent State	4
make a flow chart	of the policies and accomplishments of each presidency: • John F. Kennedy • Lyndon B. Johnson • Richard Nixon	3
search the web	for information on the Vietnam memorial in Washington, D.C. and other memorials around the U.S.	2

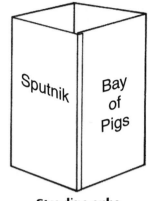

Standing cube

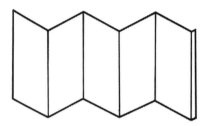

Timeline: Vietnam War

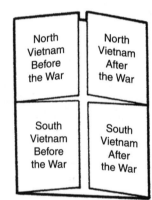

Four-door book

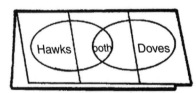

Three-tab Venn diagram

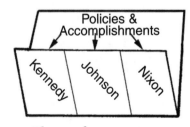

Three-tab concept map

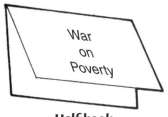

War
on
Poverty

Half book

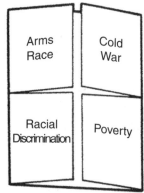

Arms Race | Cold War

Racial Discrimination | Poverty

Four-door book

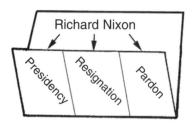

Richard Nixon

Presidency | Resignation | Pardon

Three-tab concept map

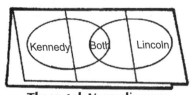

Kennedy | Both | Lincoln

Three-tab Venn diagram

War	Causes	Effects
Gulf War		
War with Iraq		

3x3 Table

America: 1950-2000

Skill	Activity Suggestion	Foldable Parts
K-LK-L	ask yourself what you know, what you would like to know, and review what you learn about America from 1950-2000	3
make a timeline	of key events in the war on poverty	any number
	of the United States space program	any number
	showing key events in the Persian Gulf War	any number
describe	four problems faced by President Kennedy in 1961: • the Cold War • arms race with Soviet Union • racial discrimination • poverty	4
locate	Cuba on a map and explain what part Fidel Castro has played in the history of Cuba	2
compare and contrast	the assassinations of John F. Kennedy and Abraham Lincoln	2
explain	the two things Lyndon Johnson wanted for all Americans--education and health care	2
outline	four key events in the Watergate scandal	4
make a concept map	about Richard Nixon--presidency, resignation, pardon	3
investigate	the who, what, when, where of one of the following: • Dwight D. Eisenhower • John F. Kennedy • Lyndon B. Johnson • Richard M. Nixon • Gerald R. Ford • James Earl Carter • Ronald W. Reagan • George Bush • William Jefferson Clinton • George W. Bush	4
	the what, where, when, why of one of the following: • the Peace Corps • the Cuban Missile crisis • "Space Race" • Kennedy assassination • "war on poverty" • first lunar landing • Watergate scandal • United States bicentennial • Persian Gulf War, 1991 • Oklahoma City bombing, 1995 • impeachment of President Clinton, 1998	4
research	how President Jimmy Carter helped bring peace between Israel and Egypt and how he made a treaty (SALT II) with the Soviet Union to limit nuclear weapons	2
write	descriptively about the causes and effects of the Gulf War (1991) and the war with Iraq (2003)	2

The New Millennium

Skill	Activity Suggestion	Foldable Parts
K-LK-L	ask yourself what you know, what you would like to know, and review what you learn about the new millennium in America	3
make a timeline	of key events in one of the following: • the War on Terrorism • the history of Afghanistan • the history of Israel • the history of the Palestinians • the history of Iran	any number
locate	the following on a map or globe: • Afghanistan • Iraq • the Middle East	3
compare and contrast	• the first years of the 19th, 20th, and 21st centuries	3
predict	what role nuclear weapons might play in future power struggles	1
investigate	the who, what, when, where of one of the following: • George W. Bush • Tony Blair • Colin Powell • Osama bin Laden • Saddam Hussein	4
	the what, when, where, why/how of one of the following: • terrorism • Y2K • al-Qaeda • Taliban regime • weapons of mass destruction	4

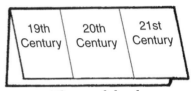

Bound book

Three-tab book

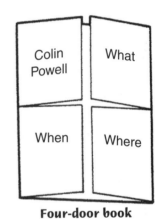

Four-door book

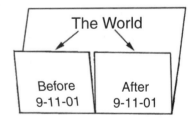

Two-tab concept map

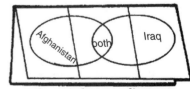

Three-tab Venn diagram

State Maps
and
Facts

Alabama

Population:	4,464,356
Landmass:	50,750 sq. mi.
	131,443 sq. km.
Capital:	Montgomery
State:	22
Region:	South
Tree:	longleaf pine
Bird:	yellowhammer
Flower:	camellia
Animal:	swallow tail butterfly
Food:	pecan
	(unofficial)
Stone:	marble
Gem:	star blue quartz
Motto:	

"We Dare Defend Our Rights"

Alaska

Population:	634,892
Landmass:	570,374 sq. mi.
	1,477,267 sq. km.
Capital:	Juneau
State:	49
Region:	Pacific Northwest
Tree:	Sitka spruce
Bird:	willow ptarmigan
Flower:	forget-me-not
Animal:	moose
Food:	salmon (unofficial)
Stone/Gem:	jade
Mineral:	gold
Motto:	

"North to the Future"

Arizona

Population:	5,307,331
Landmass:	113,642 sq. mi.
	296,400 sq. km.
Capital:	Phoenix
State:	48
Region:	Southwest
Tree:	yellow palo verde
Bird:	cactus wren
Flower:	saguaro cactus bloom
Animal:	ringtail cat
Food/Fish:	apache trout
Stone:	petrified wood
Gem:	turquoise
Motto:	

"God Enriches"

Arkansas

Population:	2,692,090
Landmass:	52,075 sq. mi.
	134,874 sq. km.
Capital:	Little Rock
State:	25
Region:	South
Tree:	pine
Bird:	mockingbird
Flower:	apple blossom
Animal:	white-tailed deer
Food:	vine ripe pink tomato
Stone:	quartz crystal
Gem:	diamond
Motto:	

"The People Rule"

California

Population:	34,501,130
Landmass:	155,973 sq. mi.
	403,970 sq. km.
Capital:	Sacramento
State:	31
Region:	West
Tree:	California redwood
Bird:	California valley quail
Flower:	golden poppy
Animal:	California grizzly bear
Food:	avocado (unofficial)
Stone:	serpentine
Gem:	benitoite
Motto:	

"Eureka"

Colorado

Population:	4,417,714
Landmass:	103,730 sq. mi.
	268,660 sq. km.
Capital:	Denver
State:	38
Region:	West
Tree:	Colorado blue spruce
Bird:	lark bunting
Flower:	columbine
Animal:	big horn sheep
Food:	rainbow trout (unofficial)
Gem:	aquamarine
Motto:	

"Nothing without Providence"

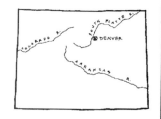

Connecticut

Population:	3,425,074
Landmass:	4,845 sq. mi.
	12,550 sq. km.
Capital:	Hartford
State:	5
Region:	Northeast
Tree:	white oak
Bird:	robin
Flower:	mountain laurel
Animal:	sperm whale
Food:	nutmeg (unofficial)
Mineral:	garnet
Motto:	

"He Who Transplanted Still Sustains"

Delaware

Population:	796,165
Landmass:	1,955 sq. mi.
	5,153 sq. km.
Capital:	Dover
State:	1
Region:	Northeast
Tree:	American holly
Bird:	blue hen chicken
Flower:	peach blossom
Insect:	lady bug
Food/Fish:	weak fish
Mineral:	sillimanite
Motto:	

"Liberty and Independence"

Florida

Population:	16,396,515
Landmass:	54,153 sq. mi.
	140,256 sq. km.
Capital:	Tallahassee
State:	27
Region:	South
Tree:	sabal palm
Bird:	mockingbird
Flower:	orange blossom
Animal:	panther
Food:	orange juice
Stone:	agatized coral
Gem:	moonstone
Motto:	

"In God We Trust"

Georgia

Population:	8,383,915
Landmass:	57,919 sq. mi.
	150,010 sq. km.
Capital:	Atlanta
State:	4
Region :	South
Tree:	live oak
Bird:	brown thrasher
Flower:	Cherokee rose
Animal:	right whale
Food:	peanut
Gem:	quartz
Motto:	

"Wisdom, Justice and Moderation"

Hawaii

Population:	1,224,398
Landmass:	6,423 sq. mi.
	16,637 sq. km.
Capital:	Honolulu
State:	50
Region:	Pacific
Tree:	kukui
Bird:	nene
Flower:	yellow hibiscus
Animal:	humpback whale
Food:	pineapple (unofficial)
Gem:	black coral
Motto:	

"The Life of the Land
is Perpetuated in
Righteousness"

Idaho

Population:	1,321,006
Landmass:	82,751 sq. mi.
	214,325 sq. km.
Capital:	Boise
State:	43
Region:	West
Tree:	white pine
Bird:	western mountain bluebird
Flower:	syringa
Animal:	appaloosa horse
Food:	potato
Stone/Gem:	star garnet
Motto:	

"It Is Forever"

Illinois

Population:	12,482,301
Landmass:	55,593 sq. mi.
	143,987 sq. km.
Capital:	Springfield
State:	21
Region:	Midwest
Tree:	white oak
Bird:	cardinal
Flower:	violet
Animal:	white-tailed deer
Food/Fish:	blue gill
Mineral:	fluorite
Motto:	

"State, Sovereignty, National Union"

Indiana

Population:	6,114,745
Landmass:	35,870 sq. mi.
	92,904 sq. km.
Capital:	Indianapolis
State:	19
Region:	Midwest
Tree:	tulip tree
Bird:	cardinal
Flower:	peony
Food:	corn (unofficial)
Stone:	limestone
Motto:	

"The Crossroads of America"

Iowa

Population:	2,923,179
Landmass:	55,875 sq. mi.
	144,716 sq. km.
Capital:	Des Moines
State:	29
Region:	Midwest
Tree:	oak
Bird:	eastern goldfinch
Flower:	wild rose
Food:	corn & soybeans (unofficial)
Stone:	geode
Motto:	

"Our Liberties We Prize and Our Rights We Will Maintain"

Kansas

Population:	2,694,641
Landmass:	81,823 sq. mi.
	211,922 sq. km.
Capital:	Topeka
State:	34
Region:	Midwest
Tree:	cottonwood
Bird:	western meadowlark
Flower:	sunflower
Animal:	buffalo
Food:	wheat (unofficial)
Motto:	

"To the Stars through Difficulties"

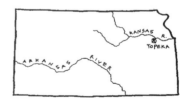

Kentucky

Population:	4,065,556
Landmass:	39,732 sq. mi.
	102,907 sq. km.
Capital:	Frankfort
State:	15
Region:	South
Tree:	tulip poplar
Bird:	cardinal
Flower:	goldenrod
Animal:	thoroughbred horse
Food:	burgoo (unofficial)
Stone:	limestone
Gem:	fresh water pearl
Motto:	

"United We Stand, Divided We Fall"

Louisiana

Population:	4,465,430
Landmass:	43,566 sq. mi.
	112,836 sq. km.
Capital:	Baton Rouge
State:	18
Region:	South
Tree:	bald cypress
Bird:	brown pelican
Flower:	magnolia
Animal:	black bear
Food:	beignet
Stone:	petrified palmwood
Gem:	agate
Motto:	

"Union, Justice, and
Confidence"

Maine

Population:	1,286,670
Landmass:	30,865 sq. mi.
	79,939 sq. km.
Capital:	Augusta
State:	23
Region:	Northeast
Tree:	white pine
Bird:	chickadee
Flower:	white pine cone & tassel
Animal:	moose
Food:	wild blueberry
Gem:	tourmaline
Motto:	
"I Lead"	

Maryland

Population:	5,375,156
Landmass:	9,775 sq. mi.
	25,316 sq. km.
Capital:	Annapolis
State:	7
Region:	Northeast
Tree:	white oak
Bird:	Baltimore oriole
Flower:	black-eyed susan
Animal:	Chesapeake Bay Retriever
Food:	crab cakes (unofficial)
Motto:	

"Manly Deeds, Womanly Words"

Massachusetts

Population:	6,379,304
Landmass:	7,838 sq. mi.
	20,300 sq. km.
Capital:	Boston
State:	6
Region:	Northeast
Tree:	American elm
Bird:	chickadee
Flower:	mayflower
Animal:	Boston terrier
Food:	cranberry
Stone:	granite
Gem:	rhodonite
Motto:	

"By The Sword We Seek
Peace, But Only
Under Liberty"

Michigan

Population:	9,990,817
Landmass:	56,809 sq. mi.
	147,135 sq. km.
Capital:	Lansing
State:	26
Region:	Midwest
Tree:	white pine
Bird:	American robin
Flower:	apple blossom
Animal:	white tailed deer
Food:	cherries
Stone:	Petosky stone
Gem:	chlorastrolite
Motto:	

"If You Seek A Pleasant
Peninsula, Look Around
You"

Minnesota

Population:	4,972,294
Landmass:	79,617 sq. mi.
	206,207 sq. km.
Capital:	St. Paul
State:	32
Region:	Midwest
Tree:	Norway pine
Bird:	great northern loon
Flower:	lady slipper
Animal:	monarch butterfly
Food:	blueberry muffin (unofficial)
Gem:	Lake Superior Agate
Motto:	

"The North Star"

Mississippi

Population:	2,858,029
Landmass:	46,914 sq. mi.
	121,506 sq. km.
Capital:	Jackson
State:	20
Region:	South
Tree:	magnolia
Bird:	mockingbird
Flower:	magnolia bloom
Animal:	red fox
Food:	catfish & shrimp (unofficial)
Stone:	petrified wood
Mineral:	mineral-lead
Motto:	

"By Valor and Arms"

Missouri

Population: 5,629,707
Landmass: 68,898 sq. mi.
178,446 sq. km.
Capital: Jefferson City
State: 24
Region: Midwest
Tree: flowering dogwood
Bird: bluebird
Flower: hawthorn
Animal: mule
Food: black walnut
Stone: mozarkite
Mineral: galena
Motto:
"The Welfare of the
People Shall Be the
Supreme Law"

Montana

Population: 904,433
Landmass: 145,556 sq. mi.
376,991 sq. km.
Capital: Helena
State: 41
Region : West
Tree: ponderosa pine
Bird: western meadowlark
Flower: bitterroot
Animal: grizzly bear
Food/Fish: spotted cutthroat trout
Gem: sapphire
Motto:
"Gold and Silver"

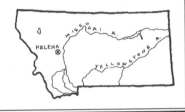

Nebraska

Population: 1,713,235
Landmass: 76,878 sq. mi.
199,113 sq. km.
Capital: Lincoln
State: 37
Region: Midwest
Tree: cottonwood
Bird: western meadowlark
Flower: goldenrod
Animal: white-tailed deer
Food: corn (unofficial)
Stone: prairie agate
Gem: blue agate
Motto:
"Equality Before Law"

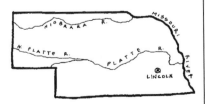

Nevada

Population: 2,106,074
Landmass: 109,806 sq. mi.
284,397 sq. km.
Capital: Carson City
State: 36
Region: West
Tree: single-leaf pinon
Bird: mountain bluebird
Flower: sagebrush
Animal: desert bighorn sheep
Food/Fish: Lahontan cutthroat trout
Stone: sandstone
Gem: opal &
turquoise
Motto:
"All For Our Country"

New Hampshire

Population: 1,259,181
Landmass: 8,969 sq. mi.
23,231 sq. km.

Capital: Concord
State: 9
Region: Northeast
Tree: white birch
Bird: purple finch
Flower: purple lilac
Animal: white-tailed deer
Food/Fish: striped bass
Stone: conway granite
Gem: smoky quartz
Motto:
"Live Free or Die"

New Jersey

Population: 8,484,431
Landmass: 7,419 sq. mi.
19,215 sq. km.

Capital: Trenton
State: 3
Region: Northeast
Tree: red oak
Bird: eastern goldfinch
Flower: purple violet
Animal: horse
Food/Fish: brook trout
Motto:
"Liberty and Prosperity"

New Mexico

Population: 1,829,146
Landmass: 121,365 sq. mi.
314,334 sq. km.

Capital: Santa Fe
State: 47
Region: Southwest
Tree: pinon pine
Bird: roadrunner
Flower: yucca
Animal: black bear
Food: biscochito (sugar cookie)
Gem: turquoise
Motto:
"It Grows As It Goes"

New York

Population: 19,011,378
Landmass: 47,224 sq. mi.
122,310 sq. km.

Capital: Albany
State: 11
Region: Northeast
Tree: sugar maple
Bird: bluebird
Flower: rose
Animal: beaver
Food: apple muffin
Gem: garnet
Motto:
"Excelsior (Ever Upward)"

North Carolina

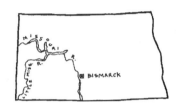

Population: 8,186,268
Landmass: 47,718 sq. mi.
               126,180 sq. km.
Capital: Raleigh
State: 12
Region: Southeast
Tree: pine
Bird: cardinal
Flower: dogwood
Animal: gray squirrel
Food: strawberry & blueberry
Stone: granite
Gem: emerald
Motto:
"To Be Rather Than To Seem"

North Dakota

Population: 634,448
Landmass: 70,704 sq. mi.
               183,123 sq. km.
Capital: Bismarck
State: 39
Region: Plains
Tree: American elm
Bird: western meadowlark
Flower: wild prairie rose
Animal: Nokata horse
Food/Fish: northern pike
Fossil: Teredo petrified wood
Motto:
"Liberty and Union, Now and Forever, One and Inseparable"

Ohio

Population: 11,373,541
Landmass: 40,953 sq. mi.
               106,067 sq. km.
Capital: Columbus
State: 17
Region: Midwest
Tree: buckeye
Bird: cardinal
Flower: scarlet carnation
Animal: white-tailed deer
Food: tomato juice
Gem: flint
Motto:
"With God, All Things Are Possible"

Oklahoma

Population: 3,460,097
Landmass: 68,679 sq. mi.
               177,877 sq. km.
Capital: Oklahoma City
State: 46
Region: Southwest
Tree: redbud
Bird: scissor-tailed flycatcher
Flower: mistletoe
Animal: bison
Meal: okra, squash, chicken fried steak, BBQ pork, grits, biscuits & gravy, corn, black-eyed peas, strawberries, pecan pie
Stone: rose rock
Motto:
"Labor Conquers All Things"

Oregon

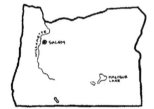

Population:	3,472,867
Landmass:	96,003 sq. mi.
	248,647 sq. km.
Capital:	Salem
State:	33
Region:	Pacific Northwest
Tree:	Douglas fir
Bird:	western meadowlark
Flower:	Oregon grape
Animal:	beaver
Food:	hazel nut
Stone:	thunder-egg
Gem:	sun stone
Motto:	

"She Flies With Her
Own Wings"

Pennsylvania

Population:	12,287,150
Landmass:	44,820 sq. mi.
	116,083 sq. km.
Capital:	Harrisburg
State:	2
Region:	Northeast
Tree:	hemlock
Bird:	ruffed grouse
Flower:	mountain laurel
Animal:	white-tailed deer
Food:	chocolate chip cookie
Fossil:	phacops rana (frog eyes)
Motto:	

"Virtue, Liberty, and Independence"

Rhode Island

Population:	1,058,920
Landmass:	1,045 sq. mi.
	2,706 sq. km.
Capital:	Providence
State:	13
Region:	Northeast
Tree:	red maple
Bird:	Rhode Island red hen
Flower:	violet
Animal/Fish:	striped bass
Food:	greening apple
Stone:	cumberlandite
Mineral:	bowenite
Motto:	

"Hope"

South Carolina

Population:	4,063,011
Landmass:	30,111 sq. mi.
	77,988 sq. km.
Capital:	Columbia
State:	8
Region:	Southeast
Tree:	palmetto
Bird:	Carolina wren
Flower:	Carolina yellow jessamine
Animal:	white-tailed deer
Food:	peach
Stone:	blue granite
Gem:	amethyst
Motto:	

"While I breathe,
I Hope"

South Dakota

Population:	756,600
Landmass:	75,898 sq. mi.
	196,575 sq. km.
Capital:	Pierre
State:	40
Region:	Plains
Tree:	Black Hills spruce
Bird:	ring necked pheasant
Flower:	American pasque
Animal:	coyote
Food:	kuchen
Gem:	fairburn agate
Mineral:	rose quartz
Motto:	

"Under God the People Rule"

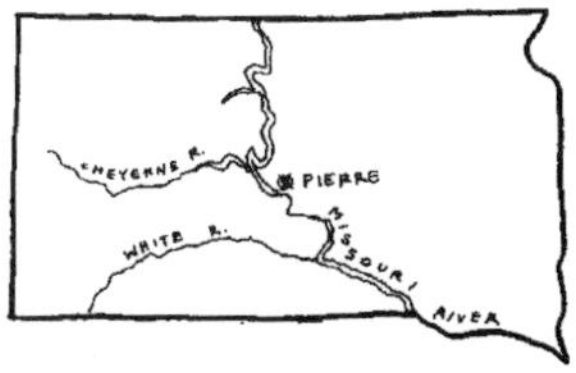

Tennessee

Population:	5,740,021
Landmass:	41,220 sq. mi.
	106,759 sq. km.
Capital :	Nashville
State:	16
Region:	South
Tree:	tulip poplar
Bird:	mockingbird
Flower:	iris
Animal:	raccoon
Food/Fish:	large mouth bass
Stone:	limestone
Gem:	river pearl
Motto:	

"Agriculture and Commerce"

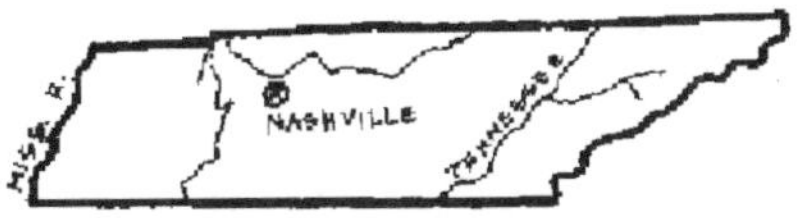

Texas

Population:	21,325,018
Landmass:	261,914 sq. mi.
	678,358 sq. km.
Capital:	Austin
State:	28
Region:	Southwest
Tree:	pecan
Bird:	mockingbird
Flower:	bluebonnet
Animal:	armadillo & longhorn
Food:	chili
Stone:	petrified palmwood
Gem:	blue topaz
Motto:	

"Friendship"

Utah

Population:	2,269,789
Landmass:	82,168 sq. mi.
	212,816 sq. km.
Capital:	Salt Lake City
State:	45
Region:	West
Tree:	blue spruce
Bird:	California gull
Flower:	sego lily
Animal:	Rocky Mountain elk
Food:	cherry
Stone:	coal
Gem:	topaz
Motto:	

"Industry"

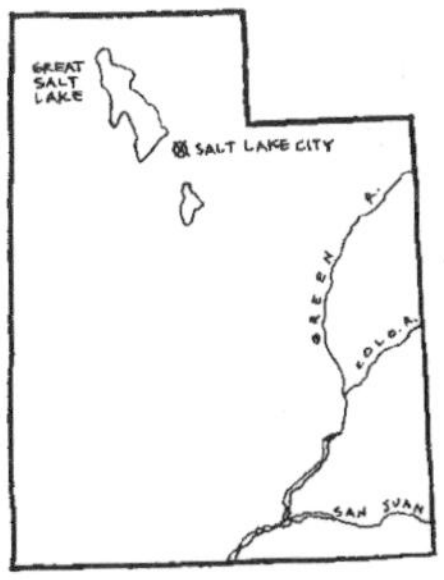

Vermont

Population:	613,090
Landmass:	9,249 sq. mi.
	23,956 sq. km.
Capital:	Montpelier
State:	14
Region:	Northeast
Tree:	sugar maple
Bird:	hermit thrush
Flower:	red clover
Animal:	Morgan horse
Food:	maple syrup (unofficial)
Stone:	granite
Gem:	talc & grossular garnet
Motto:	

"Vermont, Freedom and Unity"

Virginia

Population:	7,187,734
Landmass:	39,598 sq. mi.
	102,558 sq. km.
Capital:	Richmond
State:	10
Region:	Southeast
Tree:	dogwood
Bird:	cardinal
Flower:	American dogwood blossom
Animal:	American foxhound
Food/Fish:	brook trout
Fossil:	chesapecten jeffersonius
Motto:	

"Thus Always to Tyrants"

Washington

Population:	5,987,973
Landmass:	66,582 sq. mi.
	172,447 sq. km.
Capital:	Olympia
State:	42
Region:	Pacific Northwest
Tree:	western hemlock
Bird:	willow goldfinch
Flower:	coast rhododendron
Animal/Fish:	salmon
Food:	apple (unofficial)
Gem:	petrified wood
Motto:	

"By and By"

Washington, D.C.

Population:	57,059
Landmass:	68.25 sq. mi.
	176.75 sq. km.
Capital:	capital of the USA
Region:	Northeast
Tree:	scarlet oak
Bird:	wood thrush
Flower:	American beauty rose
Song:	"The Star Spangled Banner"
Motto:	

"Justitia Omnibus" (Justice to all)

West Virginia

Population: 1,801,916
Landmass: 24,087 sq. mi.
               62,384 sq. km.
Capital: Charleston
State: 35
Region: Southeast
Tree: sugar maple
Bird: cardinal
Flower: rhododendron
Animal: black bear
Food: apple
Motto:
"Mountaineers Are
Always Free"

Wisconsin

Population: 5,401,906
Landmass: 54,314 sq. mi.
               140,673 sq. km.
Capital: Madison
State: 30
Region: Midwest
Tree: sugar maple
Bird: robin
Flower: wood violet
Animal: dairy cow
Food: milk
Stone: red granite
Mineral: galena
Motto:
"Forward"

Wyoming

Population: 494,423
Landmass: 97,105 sq. mi.
               251,501 sq. km.
Capital: Cheyenne
State: 44
Region: West
Tree: cottonwood
Bird: meadowlark
Flower: Indian paintbrush
Animal: bison
Food: jerky (unofficial)
Gem: jade
Motto:
"Equal Rights"

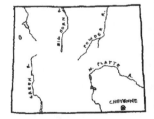

United States Presidents
(1789-present)

George Washington

1789-1797

Notes:

John Adams

1797-1801

Notes:

Thomas Jefferson

1801-1809

Notes:

James Madison

1809-1817

Notes:

James Monroe

1817-1825

Notes:

John Adams

1825-1829

Notes:

Andrew Jackson

1829-1837

Notes:

Martin Van Buren

1837-1841

Notes:

William Henry
Harrison

1841

Notes:

John Tyler

1841-1845

Notes:

James Polk

1845-1849

Notes:

Zachery Taylor

1849-1850

Notes:

Millard Fillmore

1850-1853

Notes:

Franklin Pierce

1853-1857

Notes:

James Buchanan

1857-1861

Notes:

Abraham Lincoln

1861-1865

Notes:

Andrew Johnson

1865-1869

Notes:

Ulysses S. Grant

1869-1877

Notes:

Rutherford B. Hayes

1877-1881

Notes:

James Garfield

1881

Notes:

Chester Arthur

1881-1885

Notes:

Grover Cleveland

1885-1889

Notes:

Benjamin Harrison

1889-1893

Notes:

Grover Cleveland

1893-1897

Notes:

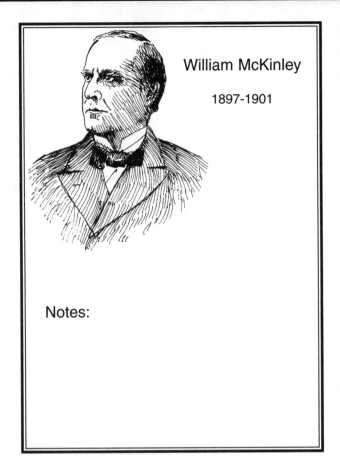

William McKinley

1897-1901

Notes:

Theodore Roosevelt

1901-1909

Notes:

William H. Taft

1909-1913

Notes:

Woodrow Wilson

1913-1921

Notes:

Warren Harding

1921-1923

Notes:

Calvin Coolidge

1923-1929

Notes:

Herbert Hoover

1929-1933

Notes:

Franklin D. Roosevelt

1933-1945

Notes:

Harry Truman

1945-1953

Notes:

Dwight Eisenhower

1953-1961

Notes:

John F. Kennedy

1961-1963

Notes:

Lyndon Johnson

1963-1969

Notes:

Richard Nixon

1969-1974

Notes:

Gerald Ford

1974-1977

Notes:

Jimmy Carter

1977-1981

Notes:

Ronald Reagan

1981-1989

Notes:

George H.W. Bush

1989-1993

Notes:

Bill Clinton

1993-2001

Notes:

George W. Bush

2001-present

Notes:

United States History
A-Z
Graphics

A

Atomic Bomb

Anasazi Pottery

Alligator

B

Bald Eagle

Baseball

Clara Barton

C

Cowboy

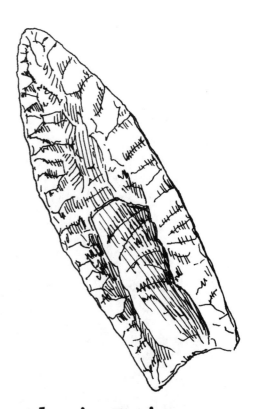

Covered Wagon   **Clovis Point**

D

D-Day

Devil's Tower

Frederick Douglas

E

Empire State Building

Ellis Island

Elvis Presley

F

Farming

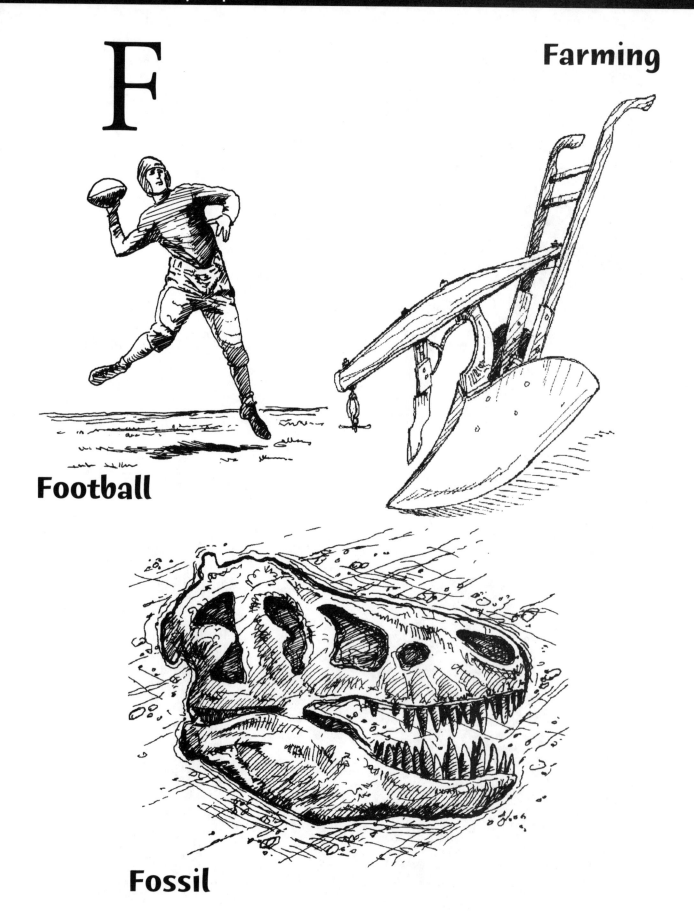

Football

Fossil

Gila Monster

Gold Rush

Golden Gate Bridge

H

Alexander Hamilton

Hoover Dam

**Hopi
Kachina
Doll**

Ice Age

I

Iron Clads

J

Judicial Branch

Jazz

K

Kent State Massacre

Martin Luther King, Jr.

Kitty Hawk

L

Lewis and Clark

Lunar Landing

Liberty Bell

Locomotive

M

Minuteman

Model T

Moose

Mayflower

N

Navajo Nation

New England Colonist

Richard Nixon

O

Jesse Owens

Oil

P

Pilgrims

Plains Indians

Quakers

Q

R

Chief Red Cloud

Ranching

S

Space Shuttle

Sitting Bull

Spanish Missions

T

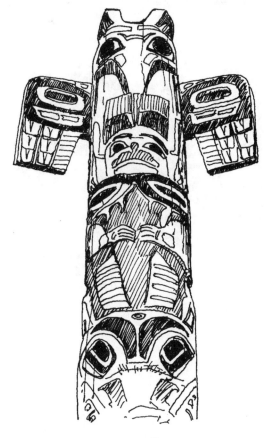

Totem Pole

Tobacco

U

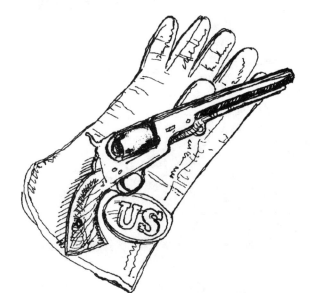

United States Cavalry

United States Flag

V

Vaquero

Vietnam

Vikings

World War I

W

Washington D.C.

World Trade Center

World War II

X,Y,Z

Malcolm X

Yellowstone

Yosemite

Zuni

Index

Index

Index

Index

Index

Workshops and Keynote Presentations

Dinah's presentations give participants an unprecedented opportunity to meet and work with the designer as she shares her internationally renowned, three-dimensional, interactive graphic organizers. Teachers learn how to make class work, projects, assessment, and note taking unforgettable visual and kinesthetic experiences. Dinah's Foldables™ can be used by students and teachers in all grade levels and subjects.

Workshops

For more information on Dinah Zike's workshops and keynote presentations, contact Cecile Stepman at **1-210-698-0123** or **cecile@dinah.com**.

Orders

To receive a free catalog or to order other books by Dinah Zike, call **1-800-99DINAH** or email at **orders@dinah.com**.

E-Group

To join Dinah Zike's e-group and receive new activity ideas, send an email to **mindy@dinah.com** or sign up on our website at **www.dinah.com**.

Watch for new and upcoming books in Dinah Zike's Big Book series!

Each book in Dinah's Big Book series is subject specific and features instructions for approximately thirty graphic organizers, 100 full-color photographed examples, five black-line art examples per page, and thousands of graphic organizer ideas for teaching.

Please check our website at www.dinah.com or call 210-698-0123 for availability of books for the following subjects:

Elementary
Dinah Zike's Big Book of...
Social Studies (K-6)
Texas History (K-7)
Math (K-6)
Phonics, Vocabulary, and Spelling (general)

Middle School and High School
Dinah Zike's Big Book of...
Science (7-12)
Math (7-12)
Texas History (K-7)
American History (7-12)
World History (7-12)